Exploring Flatwater
Eastern Maryland and Delaware

1st edition

compiled by
Ed White

assisted by
Matthew White

illustrated by
Mary Gregory

published by
Flatwater, Inc.

Virginia Beach, Virginia

Copyright 2001 by Ed White

All rights reserved. No part of this book may be reproduced or transmitted in any form by any means, electronic or mechanical, including photocopying and recording, or by any information storage or retrieval systems, except as may be expressly permitted by the 1976 Copyright Act or by the publisher. Requests for permission should be made to:

Ed White
Flatwater, Inc.
3441 Archer Ct.
Virginia Beach, Va.
23452

Illustrated maps and drawings by Mary Gregory

Library of Congress catalogue Card Number: 2001126232

White, Ed
Exploring Flatwater: Eastern Maryland and Delaware by Ed White —
1st edition
sports/travel

ISBN 0-9661672-3-6

Others books by Ed White
Exploring Flatwater: Northeast North Carolina, the Outer Banks and Eastern Virginia
Exploring Flatwater: the Complete Outer Banks

Published by Flatwater, Inc

Dedication

O Lord my God, you are very great. You are clothed with splendor and majesty. You wrap yourself in light and stretch out the heavens like a tent and lay the beams of your chambers on the waters. You make the clouds your chariot and ride on the wings of the wind. You make the wind your messenger and sit the earth on its foundations; it can never be moved. You make springs pour water into the ravines and flow between the mountains. The birds of the air nest by the waters; and they sing among the branches. How many are your works, O Lord! In wisdom you made them all. May the glory of the Lord endure forever; may the Lord rejoice in his works. I will sing to the Lord all of my life; I will sing praise to my God as long as I live. May my meditations be pleasing to him.

Except from Psalm 104

Preface

This compilation of flatwater trails is not meant to be inclusive of all possibilities. Many have been omitted. Only those of superior value have been included. Particularly, I have chosen those with exceptional scenery, an absence of or minimal litter, absence of or minimal deadfall and strainers, relatively easy access, a minimal incursion of suburban sprawl along the shoreline and a gradient that in most cases will permit travel either upstream or downstream.

I have drawn information from many sources, made many observations, and paddled many miles to give the reader the surety that these trails will each be memorable for their beauty and uniqueness.

As in any publication, one cannot be sure that the same conditions that existed at the time of writing will be the same thereafter. Should the reader discover errors please advise so that alterations can be made on each successive printing.

Be safe. Observe the safety rules. Travel with good companions and bring back lots of stories. See you on the river. God bless.

Ed White
3441 Archer Ct.
Virginia Beach, Virginia 23452
email: thewhitehouse3@juno.com

How to Use This Book

The following information will be helpful in fully understanding the material provided for each waterway in this book.

Length: All distances are reported as the shortest route possible between access points at normal water levels. Some trips must be paddled round trip and others allow the paddler to begin at one point and terminate at another. Often the paddler may extend his journey, either upstream or downstream, further than this trail guide has documented. Also, many routes are blessed with having many tributaries and creeks that invite investigation, thereby increasing length and time.

Time: Assuming there are no difficulties to impede progress, the time estimate reflects an average of two miles per hour. However, the beauty of these selected waterways beckons one to linger and enjoy, to sit and soak. I hope you can relax and stay longer. Where difficulties exist, I have increased the estimated time allotment.

Width. Waters levels at various seasons of the year can cause this data to vary wildly. With abundant rainfall, narrow channels can become wide paths making navigation less precise. However, this information, approximate as it may be, does provide the paddler with a vision of the journey. Wide areas provide open vistas and big sky where wind is always a factor. Narrow ways offer intimacy and protection. Each has its own beauty and attraction.

Difficulties: Most waterways will have few if any. If there are challenges, the reader will be alerted here.

Location: Generally, this data is expressed in approximate miles and direction from a population center. From this information the reader can better determine the most efficient travel route from his home.

General Description: I have a firm commitment to allowing the reader to "explore" for himself the intended journey and therefore have not written an extensive travelogue. However, I do recognize

v

that paddlers often have an aquatic and scenic environment that is preferable. This section attempts to describe in a very general way what type of habitat to expect.

Notes: In some trip readings the reader may find information on the unique history of these localities; in other cases, an aspect of the natural world has been emphasized. In all cases, this information is meant to educate and heighten the reader's awareness of his paddling environment.

Access point(s): Most points have space for parking and all have a reasonably good path from which to launch your craft.

Map: Follow the detailed highway routing to access points. The main roads are indicated, but other nonessential roads are left unmapped. Secondary roads, whether they be state or county, are marked "SR." Unless the reader is very familiar with the area, an accompanying high quality state map is necessary.

The recommended waterway is marked; however, in most cases, the paddler is able to extend his/her journey far beyond that which is routed. It is important to be aware that the illustrated maps are for illustration only and should not be relied upon for precise navigation. Use the legend to determine approximate distances to be traveled between points whether on water or by land.

Table of Contents

Dedication..iii

Preface... iv

How To Use This book..v

Waters On or Flowing into the Western Shore of the Chesapeake Bay

1	Baltimore Harbor.............................	6
2	Conowingo Pond.............................	8
3	Mason Neck State Park and National Wildlife Refuge	10
4	Nanjemoy Creek..............................	12
5	Point Lookout State Park.....................	14
6	Sotterly Plantation............................	16
7	Susquehanna Flats............................	18
8	Wicomico River..............................	20

Waters On or Flowing into the Eastern Shore of the Chesapeake Bay

9	Barren Creek	24
10	Blackwater National Wildlife Refuge	26
11	Chicamacomico River	28
12	Choptank River	30
13	Church Creek	32
14	Corkers Creek	34
15	Dividing Creek	36
16	Eastern Neck Island National Wildlife Refuge	38
17	Elk Neck State Park	40
18	Farm Creek	42
19	Gray's Inn Creek	44
20	Hitch Pond Branch and James Branch	46
21	Island Creek	48
22	James Island	50
23	Janes Island State Park	52
24	Kings Creek (Somerset County)	54
25	Kings Creek (Talbot County)	56
26	Langford Creek - East Fork	58
27	Langford Creek - West Fork	60
28	Little Deal Island/South Marsh Island	62

29	Marshyhope Creek	64
30	Miles Creek	66
31	Monie Creek	68
32	Nanticoke River	70
33	Nassawango River	72
34	Pitts Creek	80
35	Pocomoke River	82
36	Pokata Creek	84
37	Quantico Creek	86
38	Smith Island	88
39	Swan Creek	90
40	Tangier Island	92
41	Tavern Creek	94
42	Taylors Island Passage	96
43	Tilghman Island-Dogwood Harbor	98
44	Tilghman Island-Dun Cove	100
45	Tilghman Island-Tar Island	102
46	Transquaking River	104
47	Trap Pond to Raccoon Pond	106
48	Trussum Pond	108
49	Tuckahoe Creek	110
50	Wye Island	112

Waters On or Flowing into the Atlantic Ocean

51   Appoquinimink Creek. *116*

52   Assateague Island National Seashore. *118*

53   Blackbird Creek. *120*

54   Broadkill River. *122*

55   Cape Henlopen. *124*

56   Indian River Bay. *126*

57   Leipsic River. *128*

58   Little Assawoman Bay. *130*

59   Murderkill River. *132*

60   Old Mill Creek. *134*

61   Prime Hook Creek. *136*

62   Rehobeth Bay. *138*

63   Slaughter Creek. *140*

Appendix

Outfitters. *142*

Special Thanks. *147*

Acknowledgments. *149*

Ferry Information. *156*

Waters On or Flowing into the Western Shore of the Chesapeake Bay

Baltimore Harbor

Trip 1

Length: 9½ miles round trip

Time: 5 hours plus a little extra for sightseeing

Width: Large open harbor except for the area near town center

Difficulties: Be cautious around large ships that are underway.

Location: Baltimore

General description: Piers, container ships, storage areas, condos, marinas, and polluted water make this visually unattractive unless you like the experience of being a very small dog among all the big ones. However, the history in this place makes this a very fascinating and memorable journey.

Notes: Baltimore harbor was the birthplace and now is the resting place for the 36-gun frigate *Constellation*, the last all-sail warship built by the United States. Launched in 1797, it was the first U.S. Navy warship to capture a foreign warship. This victory took place during the undeclared war (1798-1800) with France on February 9, 1799. Near the *Constellation* is a space to haul your boat onto the sidewalk to visit the ship and enjoy the ethnic food in the area.

The American flag, still flying over Fort McHenry after a furious naval bombardment from this harbor during the War of 1812, inspired Francis Scott Key to pen our national anthem. The large flag you see is a replica of our flag at that time in history. Land on the beach to the west of the fort to visit this unforgettable site in closer detail.

Access point(s):
♦ Broenig Park. Follow I 95 to SR 2 south (exit 54), over the bridge and take the next left.

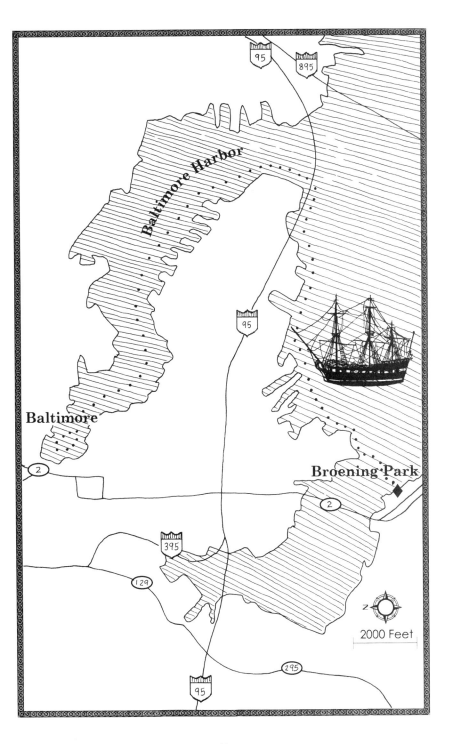

Conawingo Pond

Trip 2

Length: 5 miles round trip

Time: 2½ hours or more - don't hurry this one!

Width: 1 mile

Difficulties: None

Location: Cold Cabin Park near Delta, PA

General description: This is really a magnificent paddle among a series of small, forested, jagged rock islands in the Susquehanna River. "It looks very similar to Alaska," says Brad Nelson owner of Starrk Moon Kayaks and the local authority. The paddler is also likely to see osprey, beaver, loons and eagles in season. This trip is certainly a rare treasure.

Notes: Consider paddling upriver one mile, turn left and enter the mouth of Muddy Creek. From there paddle approximately ½ mile, walk past the rapids to the pool above to a beautiful cascading waterfall - great spot to cool down, take an invigorating shower, or frolic in the mist.

When the bald eagle, vulture, and osprey are all sighted, they can easily be distinguished by their wings during flight. The eagle soars with straight flat wings, the vulture's are also flat but held in the shape of a dihedral, and the osprey's wings have somewhat of a crook.

Access point(s):
♦ From Delta take SR 74N, cross over the creek and make a right on top of the hill onto Paper Mill Road. Go approximately 3 minutes, turn left on Cold Cabin Rd. One mile to put-in.

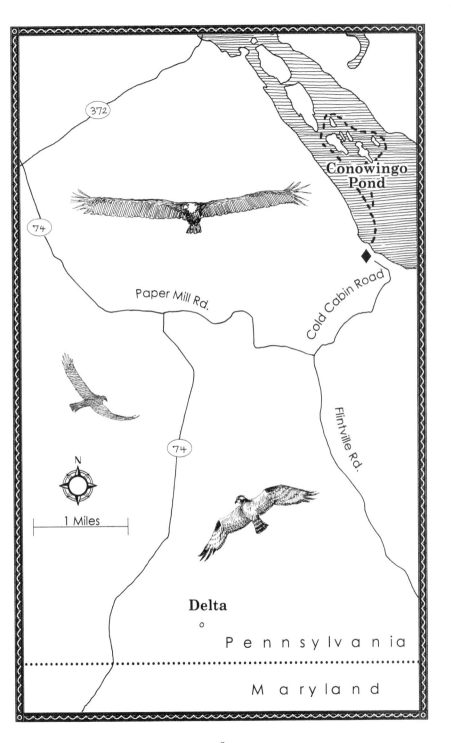

Mason Neck State Park and Wildlife Refuge

Trip 3

Length: 11 miles round trip or less depending on your choice of routes

Time: 6 hours or less

Width: Open water on the Potomac or sheltered areas of Kanes's Creek

Difficulties: Wind on the open Potomac River

Location: Near Gunston Hall, on the banks of the Potomac River.

General description: Tall bluffs, freshwater marsh, and sand beach - all may be enjoyed on this trip. Perhaps the choice treat will be the large eagle population along the northeastern shore. Also, at High Point, the paddler will discover the sights and sounds of one of the largest blue heron rookeries (700 pairs) in Virginia.

Notes: Mason Neck was the first Wildlife Refuge specifically established for the endangered bald eagle. Eagles are best seen in the late winter and early spring months. Also, over 200 species of birds have been documented here.

Mason Neck contains the largest freshwater marsh in northern Virginia.

Kane's Creek offers an extraordinary paddle in more protected waters. One may expect to see more ospreys and herons here than in any one place ever before. This is indeed a charming waterway for viewing these large birds.

Access point(s):
♦   Beside the Visitors Center in Mason Neck State Park

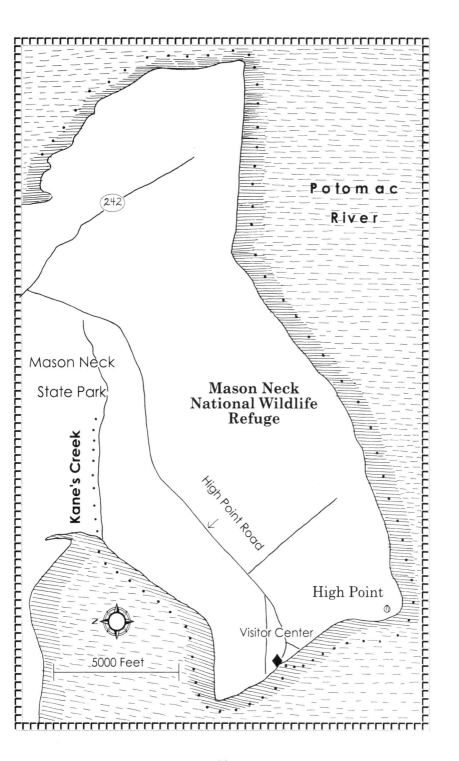

Nanjemoy Creek

Trip 4

Length: 6 miles

Time: 3 hours

Width: 20' - 150'

Difficulties: None

Location: Southern portion of Charles County

General description: This peaceful stream offers miles of scenic marshes abounding with wildlife. Its many high banks extend protection from strong winds and are nesting sites for bald eagles.

Notes: Every year in February, nearly 2500 great blue herons reappear in the Nanjemoy Creek Great Blue Heron sanctuary. The herons pair up, reinforce their nests, lay and incubate three to five eggs. By July, the young will be fledged and the colony will scatter to their summer and fall breeding grounds. The nests remain in the trees all year giving silent testimony to the activity of the breeding season. In flight, the great blue heron exhibits slow, regular beats from its huge wings. While feeding, it may stand still as a statue or walk slowly, attempting to stir up food with its feet.

The present rookery has grown from approximately 100 nests in the 1940s to more than 1300 at present. The sheer volume of their droppings, together with beaver activity, have thinned out enough trees to cause a shift in their nesting area. The nests are counted and mapped every year to track the size and shifting of the colony.

Access point(s):
♦ SR 6
♦ Friendship Landing Road

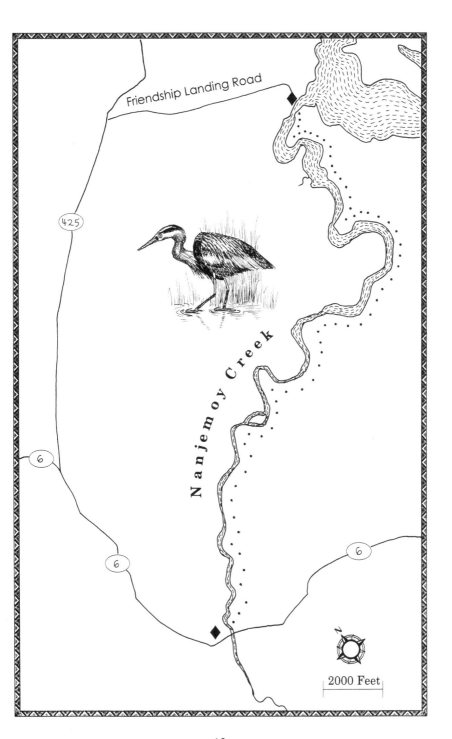

Point Lookout State Park

Trip 5

Length: 8 miles round trip around the peninsula or stay within Lake Canoy.

Time: 4 hours or less

Width: Open water around peninsula, sheltered within Lake Canoy

Difficulties: Wind if on the Potomac River or in the Bay

Location: Tip of peninsula in St. Mary's County

General description: Point Lookout is a diverse paddling opportunity. Surrounding the point, a series of rock jetties encompass the sandy peninsula. Loblolly pine and deciduous tree forests cover the higher ground behind the beaches.

Lake Canoy is bordered by cordgrass which inhibits erosion allowing a comfortably deep and navigable body of water. Fiddler crabs, muskrats, blue herons, eagles and ospreys thrive in this environment and are commonly spotted throughout the area. Prime viewing season for eagles is between February and July. The parents arrive in February, hatch their eggs, tend their young, and vacate in May.

Notes: Point Lookout is home to what was the largest prisoner of war camp in the Civil War. It housed 50,000 prisoners, 3,000 of whom died. As opposed to other prisoner of war camps which sheltered prisoners in barracks, Point Lookout was a makeshift jumble of tents and shacks with very little firewood provided. As a result, many prisoners froze during the winter. For further information, visit the Civil War Museum at the Visitors Center.

Access point(s):
♦ Boat launch at Point Lookout State Park

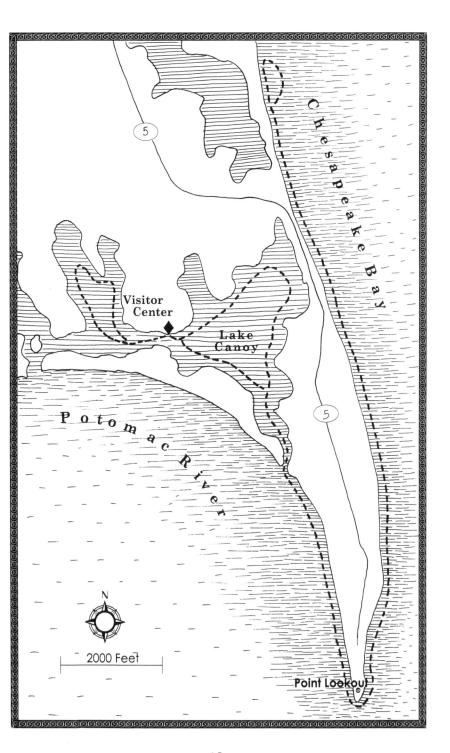

Sotterley Plantation

Trip 6

Length: 6 miles round trip from Clark's Landing

Time: 3 hours

Width: Open water

Difficulties: At the time of writing public access was closed; however, plans were being made to open soon.

Location: Western shore of the Patuxent River, near California

---

General description: Gliding by the west bank of the Patuxent River one encounters handsome hills and forests. A small white house denotes the green fields and sandy beaches of Sotterley Creek, the entrance to the plantation. While the paddler will undoubtedly enjoy the panorama from the water, try to schedule time for the landside tour as well.

Notes: The plantation is an intriguing glimpse at bygone life and is an uncommon treat for the curious paddler. Sotterley was named by *Smithsonian* magazine as one of the twelve most endangered historical sites in the entire country. Established in 1710, this stately manor is a premier example of early Tidewater architecture. Sotterly Plantation was a self-sufficient tobacco plantation, a colonial point of entry, and a busy steamship landing.

The canvasback duck - a fascinating and increasingly rare species is found here. One of the largest North American diving ducks, they dive quickly and then bob to the surface. They are also one of the fastest flyers, capable of reaching speeds up to 72 miles per hour.

Access point(s):
♦   SR 574, Clark's Landing Rd.

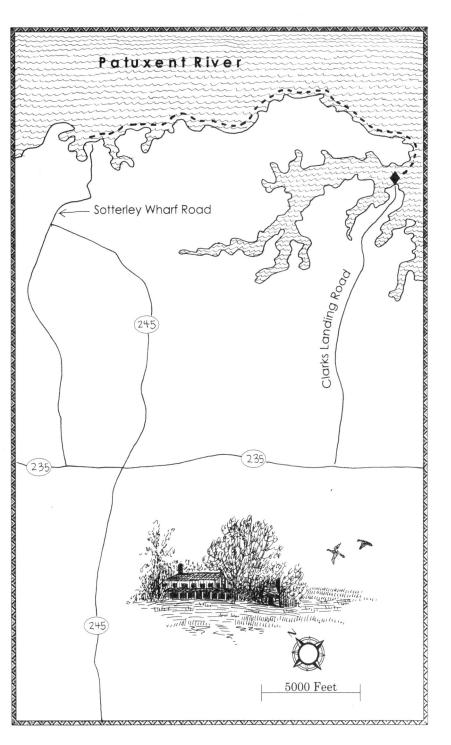

Susquehanna Flats

Trip 7

Length: 3 - 10 miles round trip depending on choice of route

Time: 1½ - 2½ hours

Width: Open water

Difficulties: Wind

Location: Havre de Grace

General description: The name "Havre de Grace" means Harbor of Grace, aptly chosen as the paddler will discover. A group of small sand and marsh islands amid the Susquehanna Flats provide enticing exploration. One is likely to observe eagles, herons, egrets and abundant migratory waterfowl in season.

Notes: The Susquehanna Flats are extremely shallow making it impossible for large boats to navigate. Once in this area, the paddler will be assured of a wide expanse of paddling freedom apart from deeper draft craft.

Nearby is the Concord Point Lighthouse, a point of historical interest, one of the few remaining from the days of sail. Established in 1827, the lighthouse served until it was deactivated in 1975.

Havre de Grace early revolutionaries penned the Bush Resolution, the last eight words of which are, "at the risque of our lives and fortunes." This rebellious document predates Patrick Henry's famous words "give me liberty or give me death" by two days.

Access point(s):
♦ The cove next to the Tidewater Grill Restaurant on the waterfront in Havre de Grace at the foot of Warren St.

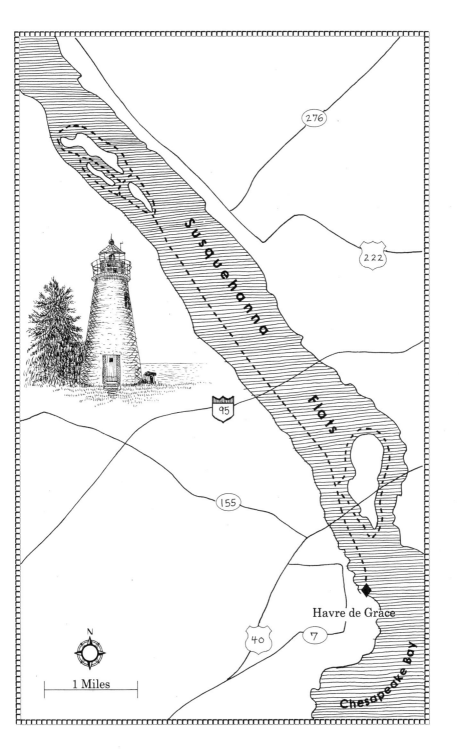

Wicomico River

Trip 8

Length: 5 miles

Time: 2½ hours

Width: 30' - 50'

Difficulties: Navigation within the channel can be tricky.

Location: Charles County, approximately 10 miles south of La Plata

---

General description: The horseshoe route between the two bridges on SR 234 travels along a narrow channel between wide marshlands behind which are farms or forested hillsides. High reeds form the corridor walls as one approaches the eastern bridge. This is a prime setting for waterfowl watching.

Notes: Charles County boasts the second largest population of bald eagles in the state of Maryland along with 321 other species of birds.

Allens Fresh has the distinction of being one of the terminals of the first mail route established in the American colonies in 1695. Mail was carried to Philadelphia and back eight times per year.

Nearby Harry W. Nice bridge is the only Potomac crossing below Maryland. Before the bridge opened in 1940, a ferry operated here as early as 1705. As the shortest route between the capitals of Maryland and Virginia, many famous Americans have crossed the river here, including George Washington. Also crossing nearby was John Wilkes Booth after the assassination of Lincoln.

Access point(s):
- Bridge on SR 234, one mile east of US 301
- Bridge on SR 234, four miles east of US 301

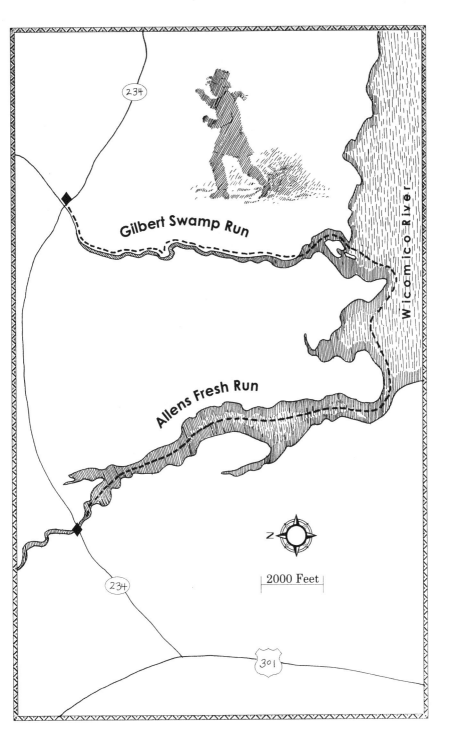

" A man finds
in the productions
of nature an inexhaustible stock
of material on which
he can empty himself, without any
temptations to envy
or malevolence, and has always
a certain prospect of discovering new
reasons for adoring the
sovereign author of the universe."
— Johnson

Waters On or Flowing into the Eastern Shore of the Chesapeake Bay

Barren Creek

Trip 9

Length: 7 miles

Time: 3½ hours

Width: 60' - 200'

Difficulties: None

Location: Between Cambridge and Salisbury

General description: A pleasant freshwater tidal paddle, Barren Creek winds in a sinuous corridor of low level aquatic growth backed by hardwood forests. Many of these trees have large growths of mistletoe (most easily seen in winter) among their branches. Access to high ground provides great places to have lunch (if not private property). As it nears the Nanticoke River, the vast marshes appear.

Kingfishers and various herons compliment the peaceful marshlands. The occasional fish flop, colorful plants in season, distant buzzards and the occasional bald eagle enhance the environs along the way.

If you wish to avoid the large Nanticoke, double your intimate experience and make the return trip to Bridge Street.

Notes: The tradition of kissing under the mistletoe (a harmful parasite particularly found on maple trees) began 1000 years ago when ancient Europeans believed the plant had magical powers to bestow life, fertility, peace, and reverse the effects of poison.

Access point(s):
♦ Bridge Street in Mardela Springs (Follow US 50 to Mardela Springs.)
♦ Race Street in Vienna. Take SR 331 to Vienna, turn left on Race Street.

Blackwater National Wildlife Refuge

Trip 10

Length: 4 miles, but this is too magnificent to take this short route.

Time: Variable

Width: Immense

Difficulties: Navigation with few landmarks, bugs, wind

Location: 6 miles south of Cambridge

General description: This ocean of water and grass almost defies description. Spend three dollars and take the scenic viewing trail by car within the Refuge to the observation point to view the immensity of this area. One should not venture in these waters without a compass. Remain within sight of landmarks (there are few) so that you do not hazard getting lost. If you can accomplish this, a trip onto this vast land of water and grass promises to be an indelible memory.

Be aware that the Refuge is closed to paddlers from October 1 to May 30. This places your paddling adventure in the worst of the bug season and can be a major stumbling block if you are not prepared.

Notes: Most of the migratory waterfowl will head north in the summer but some will remain throughout the year. Expect to see Canada geese, mallards, black ducks, wood ducks, and blue-winged teal. Other large resident birds include the great blue heron and the bald eagle. Sighting of eagles are common as the Blackwater is the center for bald eagles in the eastern United States north of Florida.

Access point(s):
♦   Key Wallace Drive
♦   SR 335

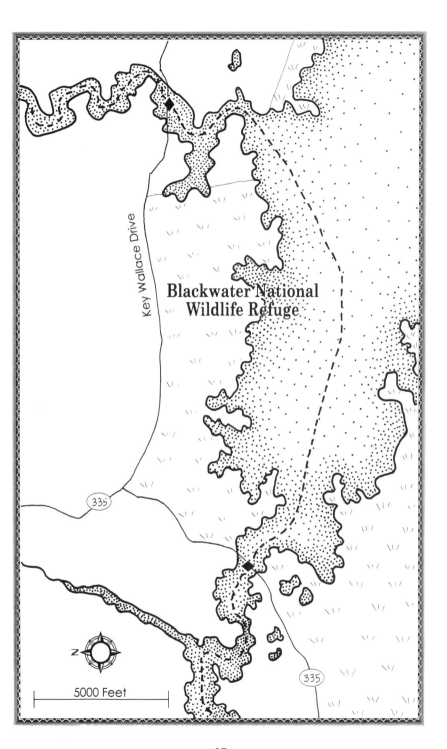

Chickamacomico River

Trip 11

Length: 11½ miles

Time: 6 hours

Width: 100' - 150'

Difficulties: Upstream portion possibly shallow at low tide

Location: 5 miles southwest of Vienna

General description: From Newbridge Rd. this river twists through hardwood swamp forest, its shores interrupted occasionally by farmhouses. Soon the marshes begin to appear and once the Chicamacomico merges with the Transquaking River, oceans of marsh delightfully dominate the landscape. Water lilies and swamp hibiscus are in profusion in the summer; other seasons host a large variety of bird life. The serenity of this landscape is a special treat.

Notes: The lily found here is called "fragrant water lily" because of its scented white flowers. It blossoms from June through September and only from early morning until noon. This plant is one of the favorite foods of the muskrat. Native Americans gathered, dried, and pounded the roots to be used as flour. Wild berries could be added and the mixture prepared as pancakes. For medicinal purposes, fresh green roots were pounded into a mash to be applied as treatment for swollen limbs.

Access point(s):
♦ New Bridge Rd. in Vienna. Follow Market St. south and it will change names to Elliott Island Rd. From the water tower travel 0.8 miles and turn right at a fork on Steele Neck Rd. Continue for 1.9 miles. At the next fork bear right on New Bridge Rd.
♦ Bestpitch Ferry Rd.

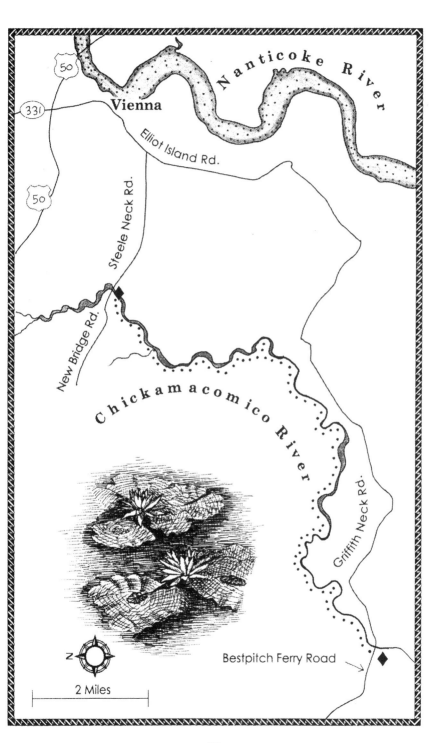

Choptank River

———————— *Trip 12* ————————

Length: 8 miles

Time: 4 hours

Width: 50' - 300'

Difficulties: None

Location: Greensboro/ Denton

———————————————————————

General description: This is a beautiful trip from Greensboro to Denton. Hardwood forests, with both high ground and swamp, as well as flourishing aquatic vegetation, flank the shoreline. This river is beautiful in the verdancy of spring, the flourishing of summer or the vivid colors of fall. Although the waterway is wider than many in the area, it is nevertheless a place of solitude and retreat.

Notes: Holly trees are frequent along this trip. Both broadleaf and evergreen, they are common as an understory in oak and beech woods. They were considered lucky and in the past have been associated with eternity and with the warding off of demons. Their brilliant red berries are said to symbolize the blood of Jesus Christ.

As a favorite tree in Ireland, folklore suggests they are the home of faries. Often holly leaves were placed under one's pillow to allow the future to be seen in dreams. Tea made of holly leaves was used for pleurisy, small pox and rheumatism. A bowl made of holly wood filled with milk is said to cure whooping cough.

———————————————————————

Access point(s):
♦ In Denton on ramp underneath bridge on Bus. 404 at junction of SR 328
♦ In Greensboro, boat ramp beneath SR 314

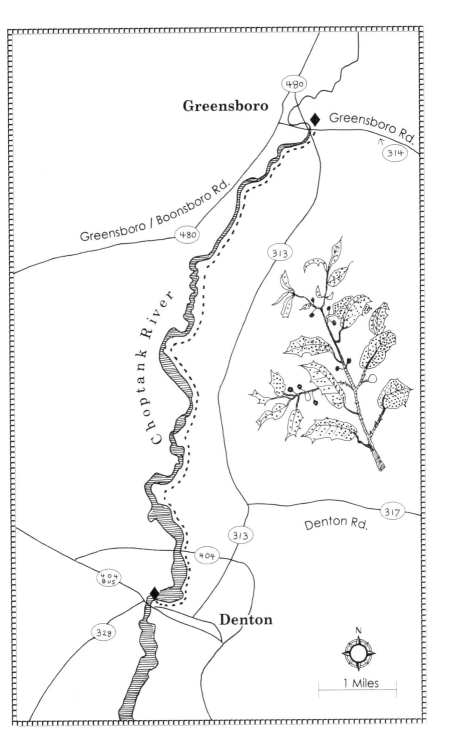

Church Creek

Trip 13

Length: 3 miles

Time: 2½ hours

Width: ¼ mile

Difficulties: None

Location: 5 miles south of Rock Hall

General description: This much less traveled creek, is quite worthy of exploration. Launching just over the bridge to Eastern Neck Island, paddle under the bridge and up Church Creek. In season many migratory birds can be seen in the coves of the creek. Bald eagles are in this area. Pass large farms and fields on the left, undeveloped woodlands on the right. Notice the huge beds of sub-aquatic vegetation before turning south. Return to Bogle's Wharf following the jagged shoreline of the island and its many coves.

Notes: Some of the grasses you might see are Coontail and Wild Celery. Coontail gets its name from its similarity to a raccoon's tail. It has densely branched stems with stiff and flattened leaves, forked with teeth on one side in whorls of nine to ten. These whorls are denser toward the top of the stem. The plant has no true roots.

Wild Celery has long, ribbon-like leaves sprouting from clusters at the base of the plant. The leaf edges are slightly serrated with a rounded tip. A light green stripe runs down the center. In season, it may have tiny white flowers.

Access point(s):
- ◆ Bridge passing over to Eastern Neck at end of SR 445
- ◆ Bogle's Wharf Landing in Eastern Neck Wildlife Refuge

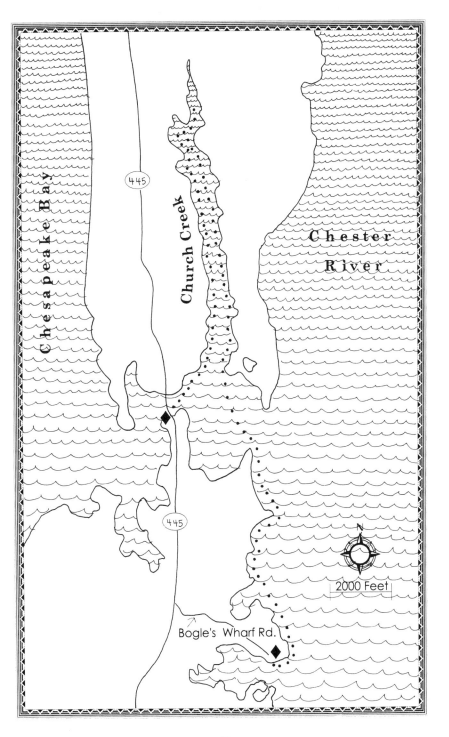

Corkers Creek

Trip 14

Length: 5 miles round trip

Time: 2½ hours

Width: 50' until the water runs out

Difficulties: None

Location: 2 - 3 miles south of Snow Hill

General description: Launching on the Pocomoke and head downstream for about one half mile before turning left into Corkers Creek. Continue upstream as far as possible, most likely about two miles. You will discover an inviting hardwood swamp forest full of maple, gum, and pine. For a shorter trip, consider the 1.5 mile self-guiding loop trail featuring the cypress forests. A superb trip!

Notes: Herons and egrets will be searching for food; ospreys and an occasional bald eagle may be soaring above; and perhaps a playful otter will follow you for a short distance.

The playful otter is a fascinating creature. It is cousin to the badger, weasel, ferret and mink and is the only marine mammal to have fur instead of blubber. Otters were once the most widely distributed mammal in the United States and Canada. Early European trappers decimated the population. By the early 1900s they had disappeared from much of their range. Today loss of habitat and pollution of waterways continue to bring survival pressure on this most playful of water mammals. One should feel blessed if given a glimpse of otters in the wild.

Access point(s):
♦ Shad Landing State Park

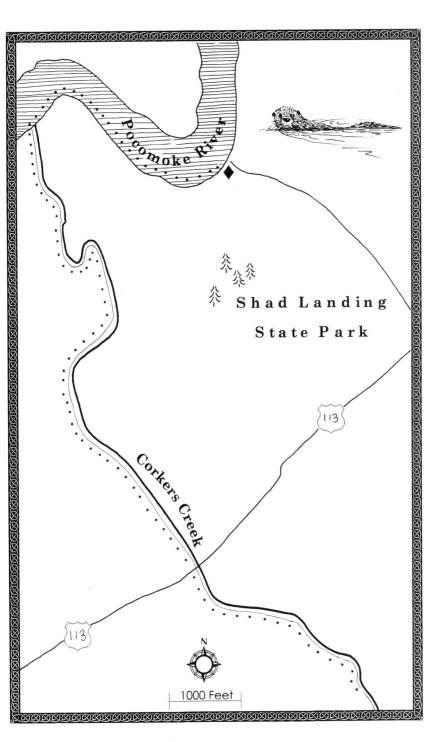

Dividing Creek

Trip 15

Length: Approximately 5 miles round trip

Time: 2½ hours

Width: 15' - 25'

Difficulties: None

Location: Pocomoke City

General description: Begin by paddling upstream approximately one mile from the launch. Turn left when you see a break in the river. You have now entered the creek, one of the most beautiful in all of Maryland. Allow yourself to be enticed as far as the depth of water will allow. This is a "do not miss" waterway.

Dividing is an enchanting, remote, winding, narrow creek usually unimpeded by trees and people, probing into the hollows and niches of the great Pocomoke Swamp. The paddler will encounter strange draping designs of pleasing greenery, fallen logs, fascinating water lilies (in summer), and the overhang of bald cypress, with its knobby knees and mangled limbs.

Notes: More than 27 species of mammals, 29 of reptiles, 14 of amphibians, and 172 species of birds have been seen in the wetlands bordering the river. Some ornithologists describe this area as one of the best environments for bird life on the Atlantic coast. Pileated woodpeckers, and prothonotary warblers frequent the swampy woodlands while eagles are often spotted over the open water. Bring your binoculars!

Access point(s):
♦ Winters Quarters Drive in Pocomoke City

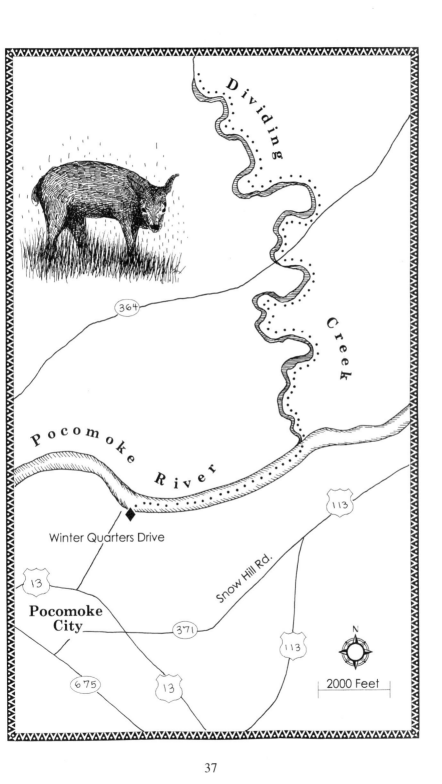

Eastern Neck Island National Wildlife Reserve

Trip 16

Length: 12 miles

Time: 6 hours

Width: Open water

Difficulties: Wind

Location: South of Rock Hall

General description: Cruise and enjoy the abundant waterfowl amongst the marshlands bordering the hardwood forest.

Notes: Eastern Neck Island Wildlife Reserve is the largest staging/refueling area for migrating tundra swans. The flight range of migrating swans is limited to a maximum of 870 miles and the birds must make a number of "refueling" stopovers lasting 2 - 3 weeks each in order to successfully complete their migration. Half of their lives is spent migrating. Powerful flyers, these birds can reach speeds of over 70 km/hr and attain altitudes of over 6000 feet.

Also seen are larger Mute Swans (identifiable by its orange bill), often mistaken for the Tundra Swans. The Mute Swan swims with its neck curved, bill pointed down, and sometimes with wings arched over its back. The Tundra Swan holds its long stately neck erect while swimming and has a black bill. Mute Swans are vigorous defenders of their nests. They will attack intruders including people and dogs. Because the territories of these exotic birds take up so much room, nesting ducks are deprived of space that they would otherwise use for nesting.

Access point(s):
♦ Boat ramp within the Refuge at the end of Bogle's Wharf Road

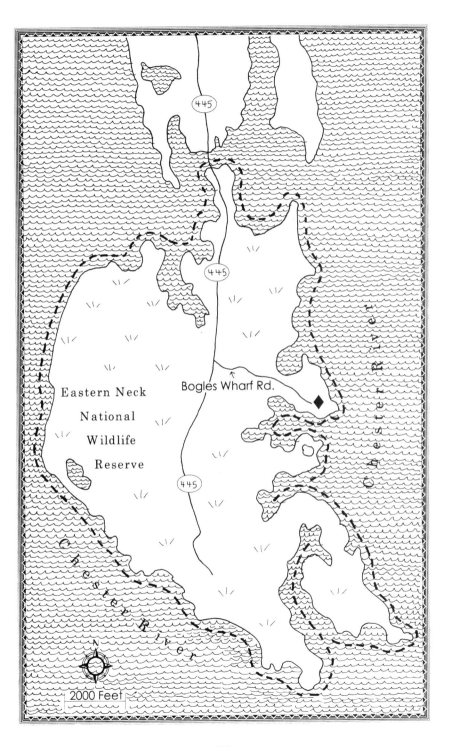

Elk Neck State Park

Trip 17

Length: 5 miles from Rogues Point to North East

Time: 3 hours

Width: Open water

Difficulties: Wind on the western side

Location: Across the Bay from Aberdeen Proving Grounds. Fifteen miles southwest of Newark.

General description: A cruise around the peninsula will take the paddler past delightful high forested bluffs, soft graceful marshlands, and enticing sandy beaches. Rarely does one experience such variety of topography in one outing. Keep an eye peeled for an occasional bald eagle, an osprey snooping for dinner, or the numerous marsh avians that populate the area.

Notes: Canoe rentals are available within the Park.

Turkey Point lighthouse, on the point, warns seafarers from a 125' bluff and is over 165 years old. The lighthouse is viewable by boat, or use your land legs for a two mile round trip hike from the Center on the blue trail.

During the 1600s wolves, cougars and buffalo inhabited this area.

A person six feet tall could wade over 700,000 acres of the Bay without being submerged.

Access point(s):
♦ Rogues Harbor Park within the Park
♦ North East canoe launch area

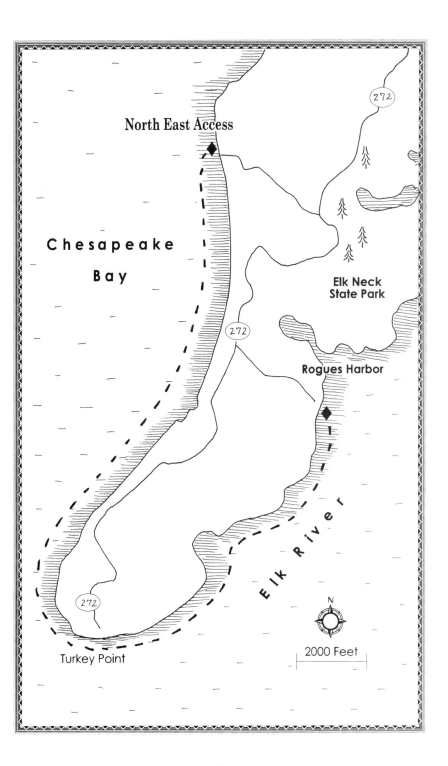

Farm Creek

Trip 18

Length: 8 - 9 miles round trip

Time: 4 hrs.

Width: 30' - 100'

Difficulties: None

Location: Near Toddville in southern Dorchester County

General description: Farm Creek threads its lonely way through perhaps the wettest area of Maryland. Ospreys, eagles, herons and egrets are common as well as many other varieties of waterfowl. Launch near the mouth, head upstream through tall reeds, marsh meadows and forests toward the headwaters which climax in a pond at Beech Ground Swamp. Enjoy the rare solitude all along the way.

Notes: The majestic Great Blue Heron is a year-round resident of this area. These birds are large, standing four feet tall with blue-gray plumage, white head, and a yellow beak. Unbelievably, they nest and mate in trees! Nesting colonies are generally located in swamp forests. Reclusive, they can be difficult to approach.

Their S-shaped neck is easily seen when they are wading, looking for dinner. Occasionally, herons capture a large fish and demonstrate a snake-like ability to swallow it whole. Their long necks have 15 - 17 vertebrae compared to 7 in both giraffes and man, and almost all mammals. Their call is a hoarse croak, especially voiced when disturbed and flying away revealing a seven-foot wingspan.

Access point(s):
♦   Farm Creek Road near Toddville

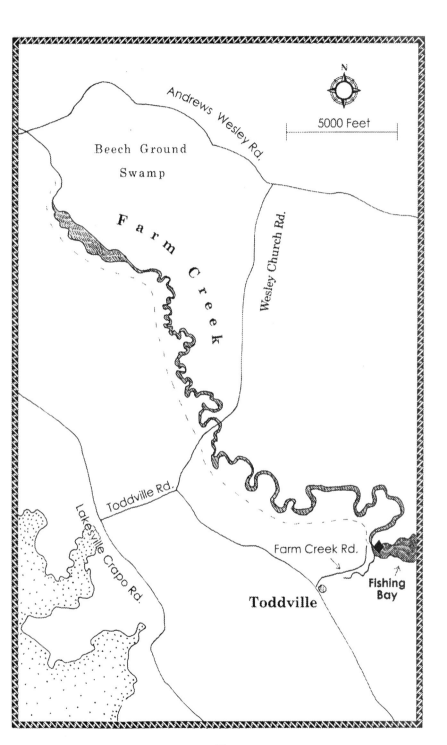

Gray's Inn Creek

Trip 19

Length: 5 miles

Time: 2 - 2½ hours

Width: 200' to open water

Difficulties: Wind on the more open stretches

Location: 1 mile south of Rock Hall

General description: Depart from the landing at Gray's Inn Creek and head downstream passing exquisite waterfront homes, many of which are being restored and enlarged. The shoreline becomes expanses of field and forest. Swans, herons, ospreys, and bald eagles as well as a variety of migratory waterfowl inhabit this portion. In the fall, the creek teems with large flocks of honking Canada geese.

Follow the western shore and venture into numerous shallow coves. Large tracts of these preserved lands are owned by the DuPonts. The DuPont estate, Napley Green, sits high on a promontory. The lands below provide excellent wildlife cover. Passing Ringgold Point one will see the wooden bridge which connects Eastern Neck Island to the peninsula. Paddle the edge of the salt marshes to the terminus at Bogle's Wharf on Eastern Neck Island.

Notes: The DuPont Company is the largest manufacturer of chemical products in the world. The company was founded in 1802 and began its road to fortune by making black gunpowder. It later manufactured high explosives and today manufactures over 1200 products.

Access point(s):
- Gray's Inn Landing off SR 445
- Bogle's Wharf in Eastern Neck Wildlife Refuge, turn left at sign

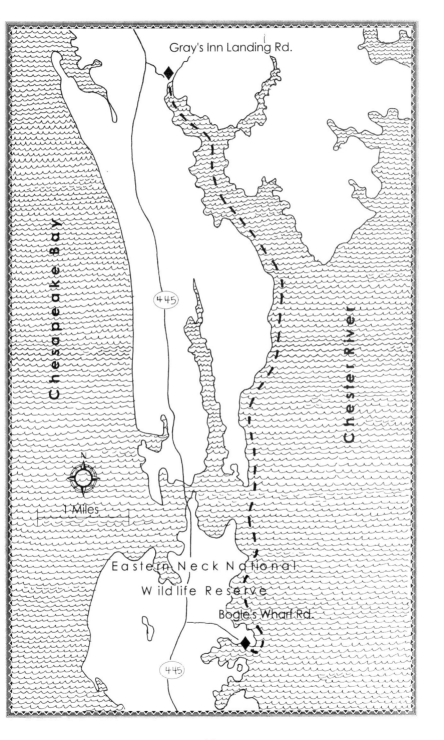

Hitch Pond Branch and James Branch

Trip 20

Length: 5 miles one way only; the current is too strong for round trip.

Time: 2½ hours

Width: 5' - 25'

Difficulties: Some downfall. Summer water levels can be very low. Cathy Ruark, Administrative Assistant at nearby Trap Pond State Park recommends paddling in late September through mid-June.

Location: Near Laurel

General description: This stream ranks among the smallest, yet wonderfully wildest in Delaware. Within this cypress swamp, one might imagine being transported eons back in time. This picturesque stream is an immersion into the vast bald cypress forests that once covered the landscape. Perhaps the "swampiness" of this landscape prevented early loggers, eager for the prized bald cypress lumber, from pillaging the land. This is the oldest bald cypress stand in Delaware and the northernmost bald cypress stand in the United States. Contained within this waterway is "The Patriarch," the oldest (700 years) and largest (25' in circumference) bald cypress in the state.

Notes: Mature bald cypress trees produce "knees" or "knobs" around the base of the tree, some standing as high as four feet. Within a cypress forest, one might see thousands of these stalagmite projections. Botanist theorize that these roots support the tree by aiding in oxygen absorption.

Access point(s):
- ◆ Bridge at spillway in Trap Pond State Park (begin here)
- ◆ Boat ramp on US 13 at Records Pond

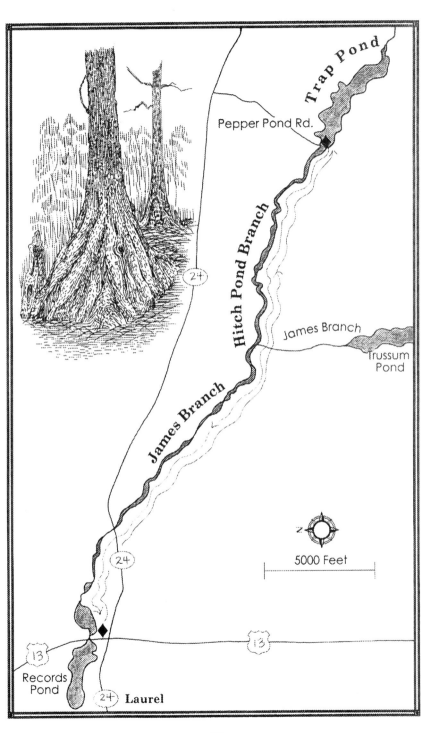

Island Creek

Trip 21

Length: 14 - 16 miles round trip

Time: 7 - 8 hours

Width: 15' - 1000'

Difficulties: Wind becomes a factor on the downstream portion. Upstream (the better route) can be confusing and sometimes shallow but navigable. Be patient and enjoy the exquisite view.

Location: 6 miles southwest of Vienna

General description: This trip has been compared to a journey through the Everglades with its vast vistas of marsh punctuated by areas of higher ground with clumps of trees. From the access point proceed to the pond by moving upstream about 1½ miles. Take the left fork at an intersection distinguished by wooden pilings on the right. This is a "must do" for lovers of the "big sky" marshlands. All the wildlife of this habitat is here in abundance.

Notes: The over-abundance of nutria threaten this wildlife ecosystem. Larger than a muskrat, they were imported in the 1930s into Louisiana as a fur-bearer. Many escaped captivity during hurricanes and have multiplied tremendously. Males may exceed 50" in length and weigh 25 lbs. Signs of nutria are feeding platforms of aquatic vegetation and debris, established trails of flattened vegetation along marshy shores, and at dusk a chorus of pig-like grunts. They will eat almost any aquatic plant, reingesting fecal pellets in order to digest food more completely.

Access point(s):
♦ Elliott Island Rd. at ramp one mile north of the Pokata Creek access

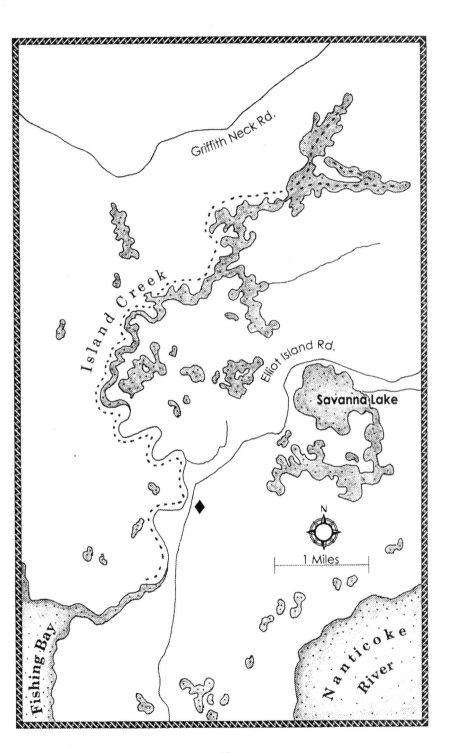

James Islands

Trip 22

Length: 10 miles

Time: 5 hours

Width: Open water

Difficulties: Wind

Location: 12 miles west of Cambridge; north of Taylors Island

General description: The closest island is a mile offshore from Taylors Island - totally deserted, and forested with loblolly pines. Extraordinary sites of erosion can be observed which over the years have separated the island from the mainland. The most northerly part of the islands has a long sand spit, perhaps the best location for rest and relaxation. You may also wish to explore Oyster Cove on the return trip.

Notes: The islands are the basis of James Michener's novel *Chesapeake.* After reading it you will ply these waters with the rich awareness of those who have gone before - the Native Americans, colonists, tobacco planters, and patriot warriors who fought the foreign enemy on these shores and waters and who even today engage the adversaries among us - persons who would seek to devalue the land, poison it, litter it, and mismanage it. Truly this Chesapeake region is worthy of our noblest efforts to preserve for our descendants the natural treasure of this land that Michener has so eloquently recorded for us.

Access point(s):
♦ Taylors Island Family Campground. The closest island is within sight, an easy paddle.

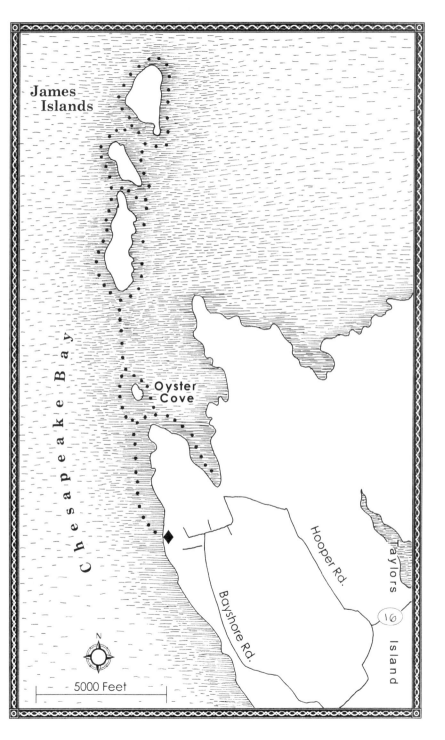

Janes Island State Park

Trip 23

Length: Choose one or more of the six color-coded canoe/kayak trails (or make your own trail) all together totaling 35 miles.

Time: Varies according to trail chosen

Width: 40' to open water

Difficulties: None

Location: Near Crisfield

General description: A paradise for paddlers offering spotless sandy beaches, protected channels, expansive marshlands, unexcelled viewing of the bountiful wildlife, and the opportunity of being among the local watermen tending their crab pots.

Six canoe/kayak trails offer a guided opportunity to explore this naturalist's haven. The wetlands, meadows and varied forest land provide nests, shelter and feeding ground for a large number of waterfowl, shorebirds and upland species. A birdwatcher's guide is available at the park office.

Notes: The original inhabitants, Native Americans, disappeared long ago, but their legacy is seen in the number of artifacts still found in large numbers on local islands. After the Indians, small farms prospered by growing a variety of food crops in the rich soil. The island also was host to a popular recreation spa featuring a boardwalk, dance pavilion and summer cottages. A "pest house" built in 1882 to accommodate quarantine cases during an epidemic.

Access point(s):
◆   Boat launch within park. SR 413 to Plantation Road

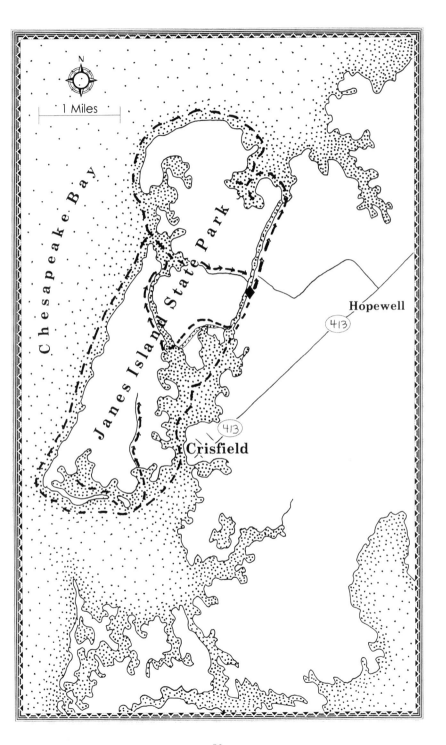

Kings Creek (Somerset County)

Trip 24

Length: 7 - 9 miles round trip

Time: 3½ - 4½ hours

Width: 15' - 100'

Difficulties: None

Location: 2 - 3 miles south of Princess Anne

General description: From the launch site, go in either direction. A pleasant mix of marsh and woods throughout the journey provides the paddler with a peaceful view and relaxing, comfortable surroundings in this relatively undeveloped and small meandering creek. Forests line the sides, numerous low aquatic water plants narrow the corridor. Cattails and colorful wildflowers (in season) enhance the peaceful scenery even more.

Notes: Some banks are cloaked in Bayberry, an evergreen aromatic shrub whose thickened and stiff leaves are aromatic when crushed. Also referred to as "wax myrtle" or "candleberry," the Bayberry plant also produces small berries, the waxy covering of which can be separated in boiling water, and has been used since Colonial times to make fragrant candles popular at Christmas time.

Bayberry bark, brewed into a spicy tea, is a popular folk remedy and was a favorite of Native Americans. It has been used in various applications to give relief to coughs, colds, flu, fevers, headache, sore throat, diarrhea, boils, cankers, and skin ulcers.

Access point(s):
♦ Stewart Neck Road - access is difficult but possible

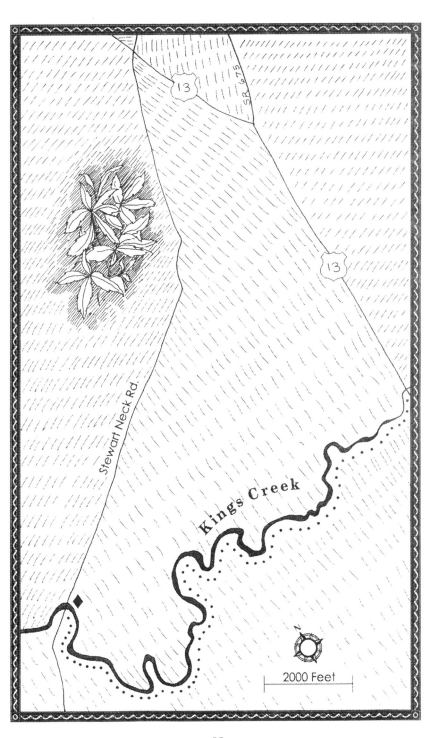

Kings Creek (Talbot County)

Trip 25

Length: 5 miles

Time: 2½ hours

Width: 15' - 200'

Difficulties: None

Location: 4 miles east of Easton

General description: An intriguing waterway, unpopulated and disheveled, but beautiful in appearance. The paddler may choose to go in either direction: downstream widens until you are enveloped in a rich and broad meadow of marshes; upstream narrows, becoming more of a swamp forest until the water ends and you can make no further headway. Cattails and other reeds remain present in a thin border. In the summer the flowers bloom wonderfully; in the fall nature's palette is resplendent on the overhanging trees, including the many sycamores that line the watery banks.

Notes: The flowering swamp hibiscus or "swamp rose mallow" is a common sight along the trip. It has strikingly showy, large, broad, white (sometimes pink) petals, a deep purple center and hides itself along the marshy banks of the stream. It stands three to eight feet tall and flowers from June through September. This plant was among the favorite subjects of Redoute, court appointed painter to Marie Antoinette and Empress Josephine. He is also often remembered for this truism, "one does best what one loves most, however humble the pursuit."

Access point(s):
♦ Bridge on Kingston Road

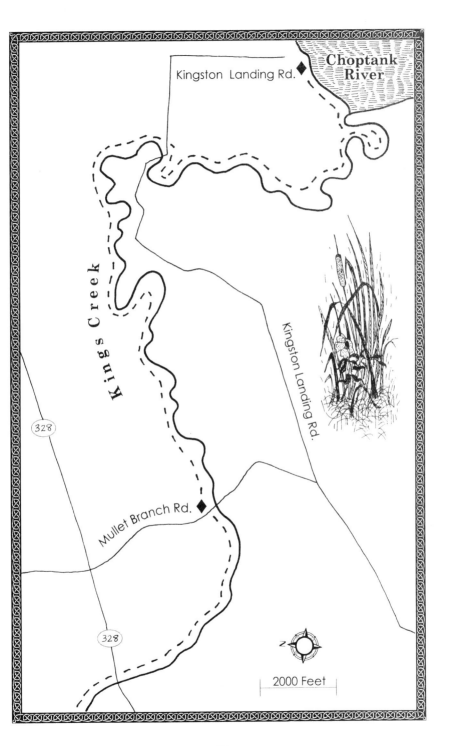

Langford Creek - East Fork

Trip 26

Length: 5 - 6 miles

Time: 3 hours

Width: ½ - ¾ mile

Difficulties: Wind occasionally

Location: 6 miles southwest of Chestertown

General description: Beginning from Broad Neck Landing, paddle up the East Fork along the western shoreline into aptly named Lovely Cove. Follow the meandering creek along a densely wooded shoreline to a basin beyond Beck's Landing and turn to head back. Return along the east shore as dense woods give way to open fields. Paddle into Phillip Creek, with its extravagant waterfront homes. Make one last entrance into small, secluded King's Creek and return to the starting point at Broad Neck Landing.

Notes: The waters around Rock Hall are home to vast numbers of eels. Until the 20th century, no one knew the life cycle of the eel. The adults simply showed up with no prior trace of the young. Eels are birthed in the saltwater of the Sargasso Sea. Soon they embark on their wondrous odyssey, taking one year to reach the American continent. Males stay in brackish estuaries, females move further upstream into freshwater lakes and streams, even dragging themselves across land for short stretches if necessary. Devouring almost anything, they will grow between three and five feet in length. After seven to twenty years, they respond to their instinctive call and journey back to the Sargasso Sea to breed, after which they die.

Access point(s):
- Broad Neck Landing. SR 446 (Broad Neck Road) to end

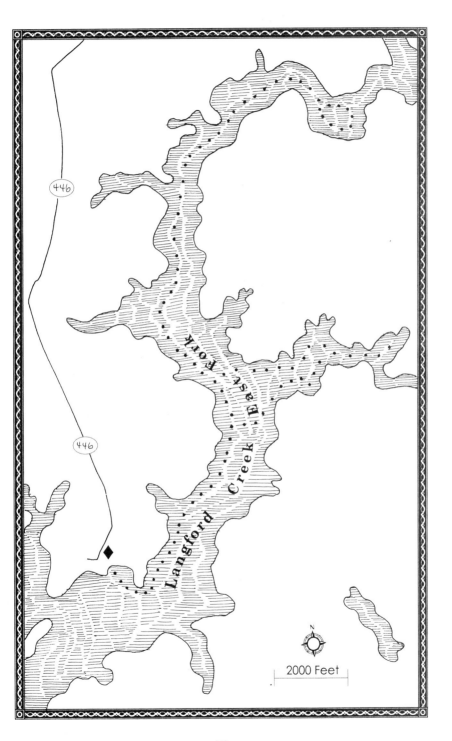

Langford Creek - West Fork

Trip 27

Length: 7 miles

Time: 3½ hours

Width: ¼ mile to 1½ miles (near Cacaway Island)

Difficulties: Wind

Location: 6 miles southwest of Chestertown

General description: Beginning at Shipyard Landing, paddle downstream past osprey nests and abandoned duck blinds on the protected creek. Occasionally, bald eagles may be seen along the eastern side. There is a small beach on the eastern side where you may wish to stop for a rest. Venture into Davis Creek and glide past the graceful sailboats on their moorings. Crossing the shallows off Drum Point, turn toward Long Cove and slip past the quaint Rock Hall Yacht Club and conclude at the working marina at Long Cove. Another option is to bear left at Shipyard Landing and follow the creek as it becomes a wandering stream through tidal marsh - like a scene from "The African Queen."

Notes: Osprey, also known as "fish hawks," are noted for their feet-first plunge into shallow water to catch fish. After the bird catches the fish, it arranges its prey in its talons to face forward to reduce drag. These predators normally nest in the same place every year (usually dead trees), adding to their nests which can weigh more than 200 pounds.

Access point(s):
- Shipyard Landing. From Rock Hall take SR 20N, turn right on Shipyard Lane.
- Long Cove. From Rock Hall follow SR 288 to terminus.

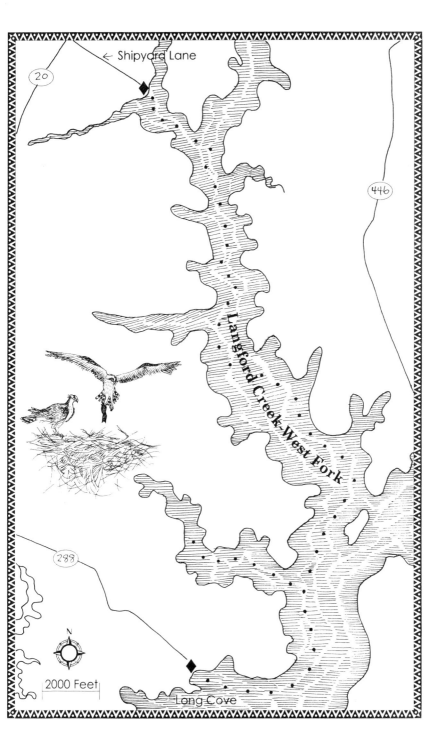

Little Deal Island/South Marsh Island

Trip 28

Length: 4 miles, add 8 or more miles for a visit to South Marsh.

Time: 2 hours, add 4 or more for South Marsh Island.

Width: Open water

Difficulties: Wind

Location: 21 miles west of Princess Anne at the end of SR 363

General description: The Deal Islands are a seemingly limitless expanse of tidal marsh. Also of interest is the presence of skipjacks, a single-masted working sailboat from yesteryear. Today only a few are still operable to dredge for oysters in the winter.

Notes: The Deal Islands rank among the best places in Maryland to watch and photograph ducks and geese. Many species of waterfowl nest, feed and migrate through this area. The Deal Islands also support one of the largest concentrations in the state of herons, egrets and ibis. Maryland's only breeding population of black-necked stilts thrives here. The rare European widgeon, a type of duck, is frequently seen in the large flocks of American widgeons that spend the winter in Maryland. Widgeons ride high in the water, picking at the surface; in flight they are recognized by large white patches on their forewing.

For more adventure, take an extended trip to South Marsh Island Wildlife Management Area. The marsh was once a convenient hiding place for "picaroons," or pirates, who harassed unprotected American ships during the Revolutionary War.

Access point(s):
♦ End of SR 363 at boat ramp in Wenona Harbor

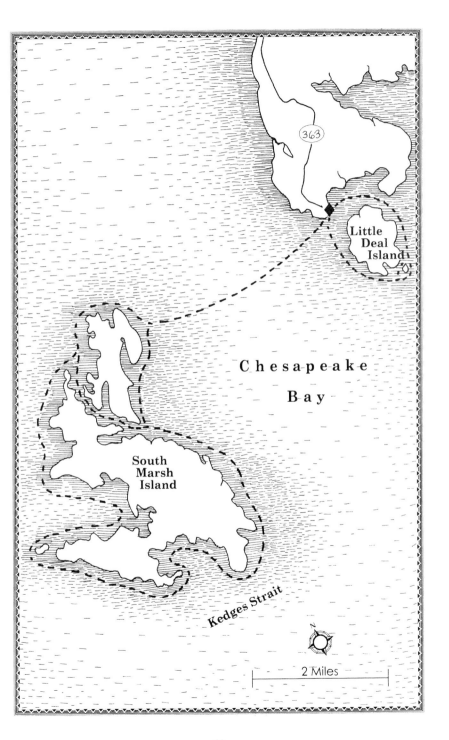

Marshyhope Creek

Trip 29

Length: 9½ miles

Time: 5 hours

Width: 20' - 30'

Difficulties: Occasional deadfall

Location: 3 - 5 miles north northeast of Federalsburg

General description: This intriguing creek cuts a narrow winding path through freshwater marsh and hardwood swamp forest. While the paddler may encounter deadfall along the way, alternate bypass routes are often possible. For some of us, the obstructions add to the challenge. Check out the side channels, they are great places in which to poke around.

Notes: Forming the western boundary of the Idlewild Wildlife Management Area, Marshyhope Creek is among the least spoiled waterways in the Chesapeake Bay region. Bald eagles, ospreys, great blue herons, varieties of hawks, and turkeys are five of the year-round residents. Migrating waterfowl are regular visitors. The spring and fall are the best times to encounter a large variety of songbirds as they also journey north and south in season. A sharp eye will catch the beautiful colors of scarlet tanagers, woodpeckers, and bluebirds.

The Marshyhope is also home to beavers, often seen busily working on their dams or winter food stores.

Access point(s):
- SR 404 (Look for the dirt road access on the east side of the creek immediately at the guard rail by the bridge.)
- Maryland SR 318, public marina in Federalsburg

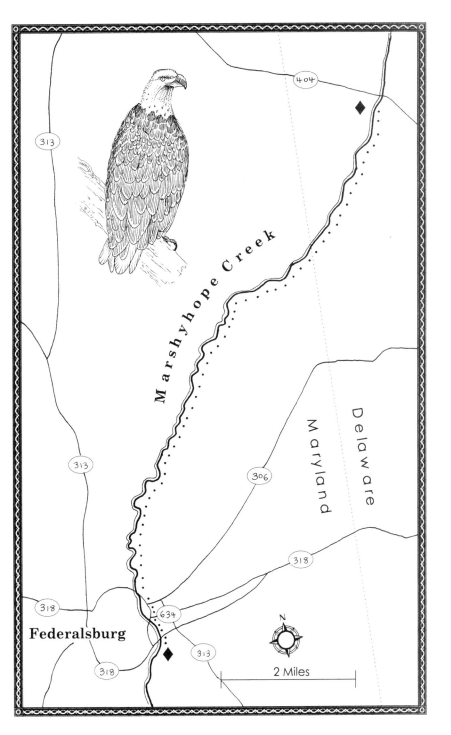

Miles Creek

Trip 30

Length: 5½ miles round trip

Time: 3 hours

Width: 15' - 250'

Difficulties: Affected by tides, travel at high tide if possible.

Location: 5 miles southeast of Easton

General description: From the access, the upstream choice will find this creek gradually narrowing as it winds through the forested high banks. The distance of the journey upstream will be determined by the tide; nevertheless, go as far as you can for a most rewarding trip. Turning downstream, the creek widens to over 200' as it follows a convoluted path through expansive wetlands. It is approximately two miles to the intersection with the Choptank River. This is a beautiful paddle, another "must do."

Notes: A journey on this tributary of the Choptank places one in the middle of the first chapters of James Michener's *Chesapeake*. He describes the Choptank Indians who first inhabited this region as peace loving, gentle, and smaller in stature than their neighbors, the Nanticokes, who were extremely fond of raiding Choptank territory. Rather than engage in warfare and risk the certain loss of life, the Choptanks would retreat to the marshlands as invaders approached, allowing the plundering of possessions that were easily replaced. After a few days the invaders would leave and the Choptanks would return to reoccupy their land and resume their peaceful coexistence with each other and the land they loved.

Access point(s):
♦ Bridge at Bruceville Road

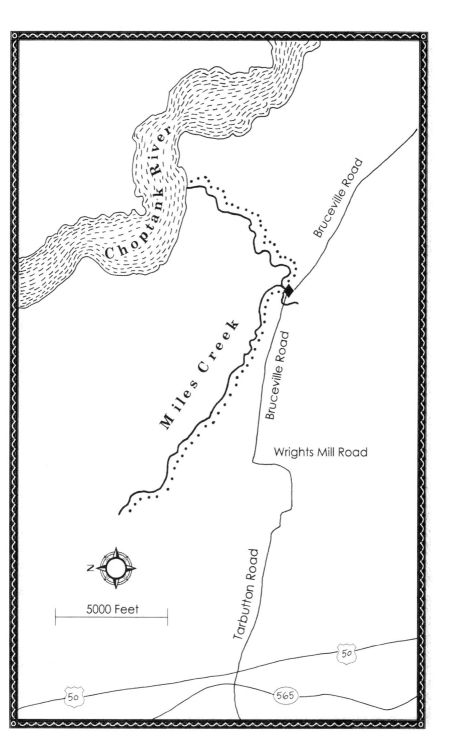

Monie Creek

Trip 31

Length: 5 miles, add more if continuing into Deal Island Wildlife Management Area.

Width: 20' - 150'

Time: 2½ hours or more (take plenty on this one)

Difficulties: None

Location: 3 - 5 miles west of Princess Anne

General description: This sinuous, enchanting creek can be done as a one way from Mount Vernon Rd., or as a round trip from Drawbridge Rd. into the saltwater marshes of Deal Island Wildlife Management Area. Some consider this downstream portion into Monie Bay the prettiest part of the waterway.

Notes: The Monie Bay area, woven by tidal creeks, is a shallow salt marsh joining dry land and the open waters of the Chesapeake Bay. These waters supply favorite food for migrating waterfowl, especially widgeon, black ducks, green-winged teal and coots.

A keen eye can observe bald eagles, osprey and northern harriers overhead as they search for nourishment. Shoreline birds forage in the shallows for edibles. Fiddler crabs scurry for protection in the mudbanks. Marsh periwinkles (½"), easily mistaken for part of the cordgrass, can be seen climbing the grass eating the algae. Burrowed beneath the mud are the worms, clams and mud shrimp that endlessly filter food particles from the water passing over them.

Access point(s):
♦ Mount Vernon Rd., SR 362
♦ Drawbridge Rd.

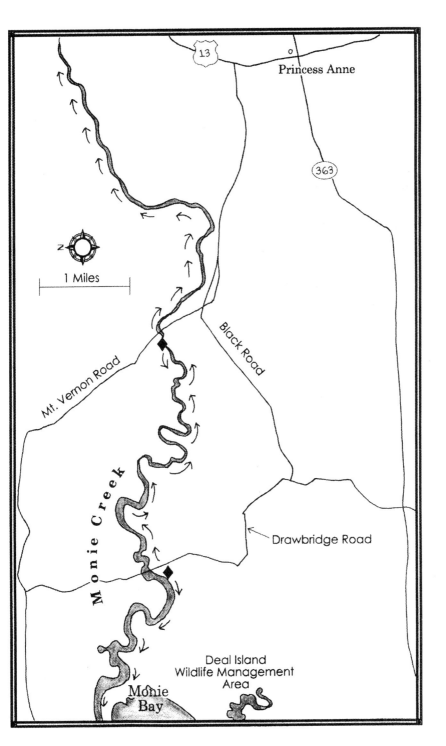

Nanticoke River

Trip 32

Length: 9½ miles

Time: 5 hours

Width: 20' - 100'

Difficulties: Deadfall in places

Location: Between Seaford and Bridgeville

General description: Downriver the Nanticoke spreads across the marshland; the upper reach offers a narrower and more private passage through freshwater woodland swamp. If one can arrange to journey during high water, the deadfalls are less troublesome; nonetheless, they make for interesting navigation.

Notes: The Nanticoke was found by Captain John Smith in 1608 during his exploration of the rivers of the Chesapeake Bay. He encountered the Nantaquak, their translated name meaning "those who ply the tidal stream." These Indians were accomplished canoeists and therefore did not lead an isolated life. Smith called them "the best Merchants" of all other tribes in the region.

During the 19th century, the Nanticoke supported a thriving shipbuilding industry. Schooners and shad barges were constructed from the rot-resistant cedar along its banks. The Nanticoke still has some of the northernmost stands of bald cypress trees on the Atlantic coast.

Access point(s):
- Rifle Range Road (SR 545). Turn east 0.4 miles north of junction of 13/13A/404.
- US 13 in Seaford

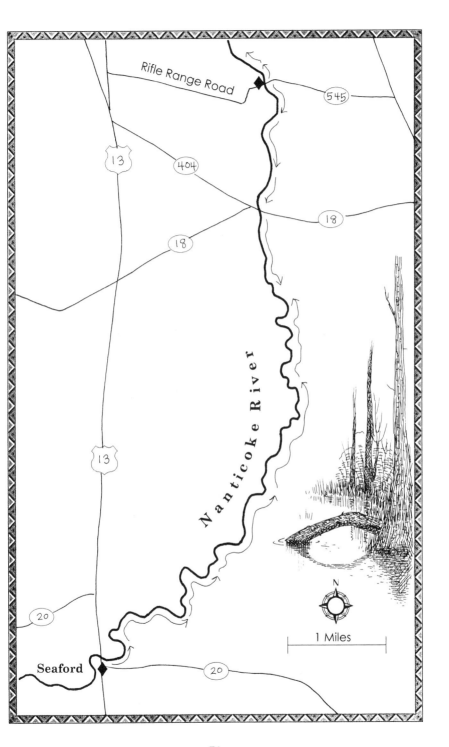

Nassawango Creek

Trip 33

Length: 7 miles. Begin at SR 12 and paddle to the mouth, then return 1 mile to Nassawango Rd.

Time: 3½ hours

Width: 10' - 500'

Difficulties: Fallen trees upstream

Location: 7 miles northwest of South Hill

General description: This is a beauty! At the onset, water flows swiftly through a deep, enchanting, hardwood swamp forest. Toward the terminus, surface water plants comprise an exquisite carpet along the water's edge. This is an unrefined, rugged environment requiring challenging navigation over, through, and in between fallen trees - a personally demanding paddle, exceedingly pretty, and saturated with delightful scenery.

Notes: The Nassawango flows through reportedly haunted Furnace Town. Once a thriving foundry town, it lost its economic viability and declined until one solitary slave, Sampson Hat, remained even though he was free to go. Declaring he wanted to be buried there, he died at the age of 107 and his body was moved elsewhere. To this day the visage of a tall black man is reportedly seen among the museum restorations.

Access point(s):
♦   SR 12
♦   Red House Rd. off SR 12
♦   Nassawongo Rd.

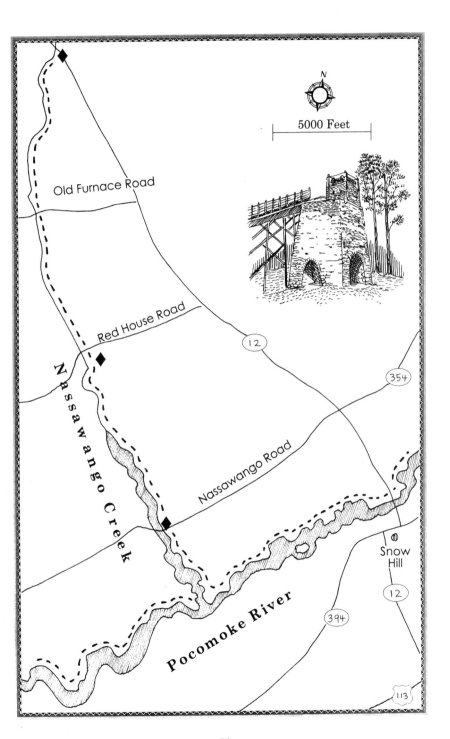

"The moment may be temporary,

but the memory is forever."

—Bud Meyer

Regional Map Guide

1. Baltimore Harbor
2. Conowingo Pond
3. Mason Neck STATE PK & WR
4. Nanjemoy Creek
5. Point Lookout STATE PARK
6. Sotterly Plantation
7. Susquehanna Flats
8. Wicomico River
9. Barren Creek
10. Blackwater NWR
11. Chicamacomico River
12. Choptank River
13. Church Creek
14. Corkers Creek
15. Dividing Creek
16. Eastern Neck Island NWR
17. Elk Neck State Park
18. Farm Creek
19. Gray's Inn Creek
20. Hitch Pond & James Br.
21. Island Creek
22. James Island
23. Janes Island STATE PARK
24. Kings Creek (SOMERSET)
25. Kings Creek (TALBOT)
26. Langford Creek EAST FORK
27. Langford Creek WEST FORK
28. Little Deal/So. Marsh Is.
29. Marshyhope Creek
30. Miles Creek
31. Monie Creek
32. Nanticoke River
33. Nassawango Creek
34. Pitts Creek
35. Pocomoke River
36. Pokata Creek
37. Quantico Creek
38. Smith Island
39. Swan Creek

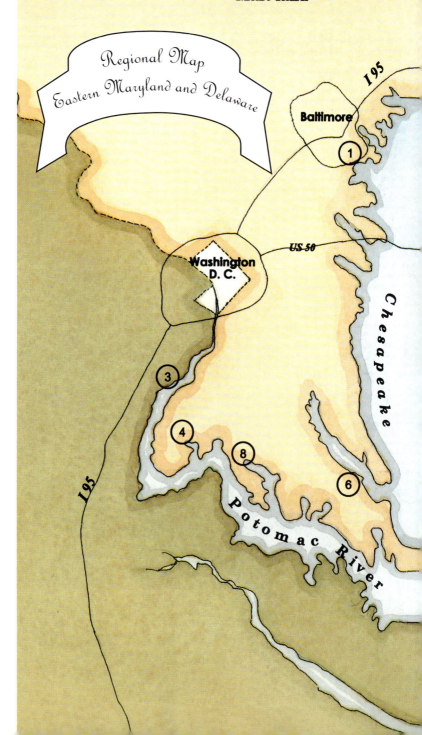

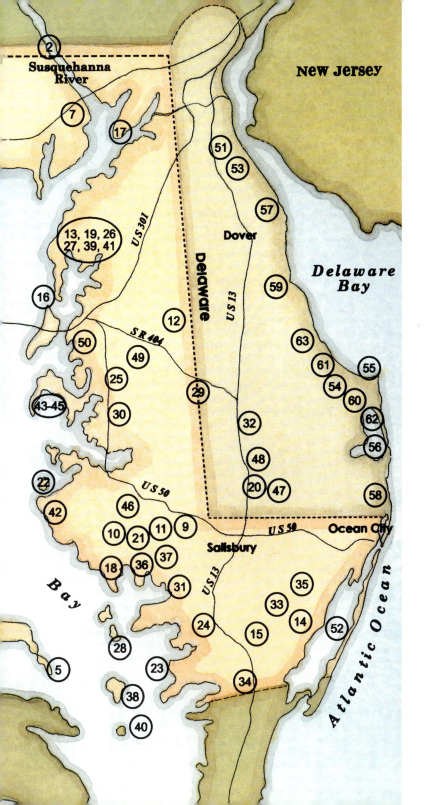

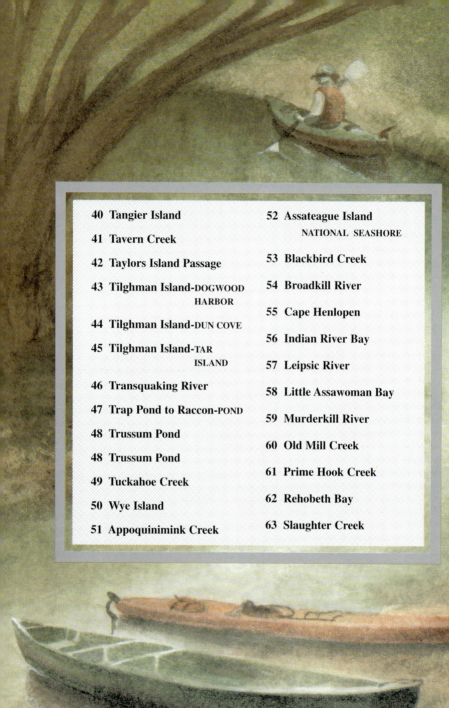

40 Tangier Island

41 Tavern Creek

42 Taylors Island Passage

43 Tilghman Island-DOGWOOD HARBOR

44 Tilghman Island-DUN COVE

45 Tilghman Island-TAR ISLAND

46 Transquaking River

47 Trap Pond to Raccon-POND

48 Trussum Pond

48 Trussum Pond

49 Tuckahoe Creek

50 Wye Island

51 Appoquinimink Creek

52 Assateague Island NATIONAL SEASHORE

53 Blackbird Creek

54 Broadkill River

55 Cape Henlopen

56 Indian River Bay

57 Leipsic River

58 Little Assawoman Bay

59 Murderkill River

60 Old Mill Creek

61 Prime Hook Creek

62 Rehobeth Bay

63 Slaughter Creek

" Enjoy the little things, for one day you may look back and realize they were the big things. "

– Robert Brault

Pitts Creek

Trip 34

Length: 5 miles

Time: 2½ hours

Width: 30' - 150'

Difficulties: None

Location: 5 - 6 miles south of Pocomoke City on MD/VA line

General description: From Wagram Rd. head upstream as far as you are able through picturesque, placid freshwater marsh. Enjoy the wildflowers in blossom in summer. When choosing the downstream course, you will travel through the intimate, serene and beautiful swamp forest; especially magnificent in the brilliant colors of emerging verdant spring green or the full palette of fall. If entering from Bell Rd., do not be discouraged by the wide appearance - this is the Pocomoke River. Turn right and in approximately one half mile you will enter Pitts Creek. This is a beautiful trip!

Notes: There are waterfowl aplenty in this creek, especially various species of marsh ducks. These ducks stand on their head to secure their food and take flight directly into the air.

Particularly observe black ducks, common in this area. On the water they are mallard-size, black or dark-brown in color. The black duck even quacks like a mallard. In contrast, the male mallard is distinguished by a green head, set off by a white neck ring. In flight the black duck is very dark with flashing white wing linings.

Access point(s):
♦   SR 707 Wagram Rd.
♦   SR 804 Bell Rd.

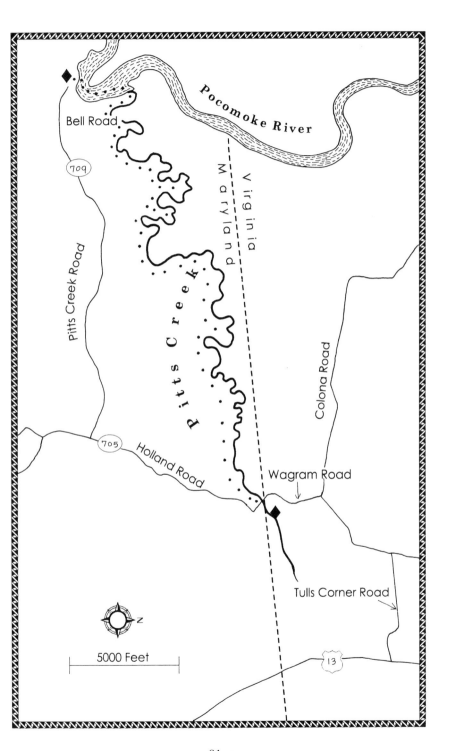

Pocomoke River

Trip 35

Length: See the map and choose from a variety of possibilities between access points.

Time: Dependant upon route chosen

Width: 15' - 60'

Difficulties: Occasional deadfall

Location: Near Snow Hill

General description: Banks lined with gnarled cypress trees provide an eerie solitude under their intertwining branches. Upstream, the coffee-colored water is hidden under a tunnel-like canopy, rendering this swampy trail a delight for those seeking silence and absence from distractions. Proceeding downstream, the river widens gradually, but the beauty never diminishes. Don't miss this one!

Notes: The *Baltimore Sun* writes, "...those who know the Pocomoke River say there is nothing like it in this part of the world. Lush with wildlife, swampy and dark, there is a mystique about the river that gives each new visitor the sense that he is the first to explore its waters."

Deserting Union and Confederate troops as well as underground railroaders, bootleggers, pirates and smugglers have all found refuge in the river's twisted paths.

Access point(s):
♦ SR 346
♦ Whiton Crossing Road
♦ Porters Crossing Road
♦ Snow Hill City Park

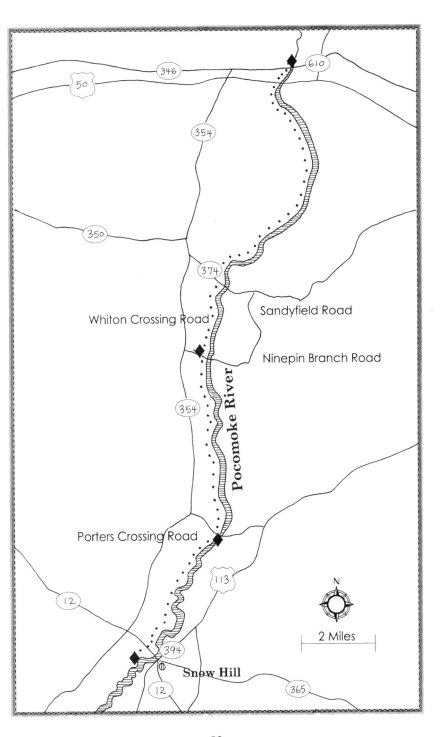

Pokata Creek

Trip 36

Length: 8 miles round trip

Time: 4 hours

Width: 10' - 100'

Difficulties: None

Location: West of Salisbury flowing through Fishing Bay WMA

General description: Like its nearby cousin Island Creek, these are "the Everglades of Maryland" - beautiful, vast, open sky, filled with wildlife above and below the water. Upstream travels a sinuous path through high marsh grass. This curtain gradually thins, offering the traveler beautiful vistas of salt marsh meadows in all directions. Eventually, the Pokata becomes the very shallow Little Savanna Lake. It is unlikely to be deep enough to navigate. Downstream, this waterway continues through the marshes as it bisects the Management Area.

Notes: Along this route you will find both geese and ducks. Ducks are the largest group of waterfowl and also the most diverse. The characteristics generally held in common by ducks when compared to geese and swans are their small body size, shorter necks, narrower wings which are more pointed, and more rapid wing beats.

On this trip, look for scaup, a common diving duck of this area. Scaup are the only ducks with broad white stripes on the trailing edge of their wings. Viewed on the water, they are black on both ends with white in the middle.

Access point(s):
◆ Pullover on Elliott Island Rd. 0.7 mile south of Fishing Bay WMA sign

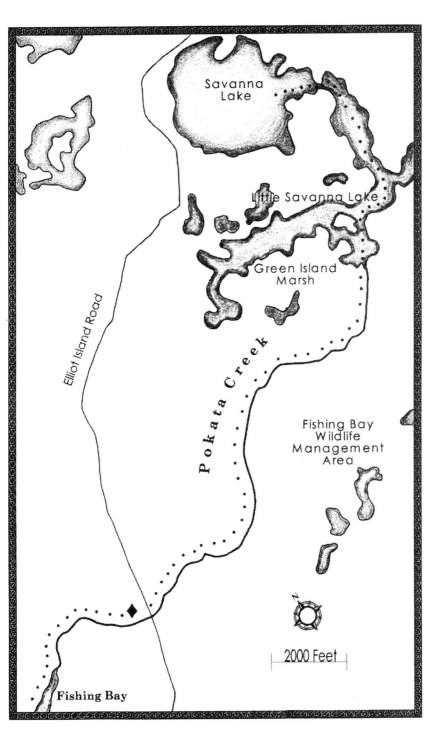

Quantico Creek

Trip 37

Length: 10 miles round trip

Time: 5 hours

Width: 15' - 200'

Difficulties: Some deadfall at the beginning. High tide helps at the launch point.

Location: 9 miles west of Salisbury

General description: If you like challenges, this is the place for you, especially at the launch. The hardy adventurer will have fun on the narrow and forested first mile. Continuing downstream, this creek widens considerably. Behind the marsh are banks of stately, tall, pine woods. The lower portions form the border of the Nanticoke River Wildlife Management Area.

Notes: The website for the Management Area reports that barn owls can be seen in the marshes. The barn owl is the only owl with a white heart-shaped face. Owls are distinguished on the wing by their light moth-like flight. Farmers are attracted to the barn owl's ability to control rodents better than traps, poison, or cats, at no cost. Young owls will eat the equivalent of a dozen mice per night. Adult barn owls kill and consume the equivalent of one large rat or gopher per night. These owls consume twice as much food for their weight as other owls. Barn owls are prolific breeders and will produce large broods once or even twice per year; however, the number of barn owls in an area is limited by both prey base and suitable nesting sites.

Access point(s):
♦   SR 347, difficult but possible

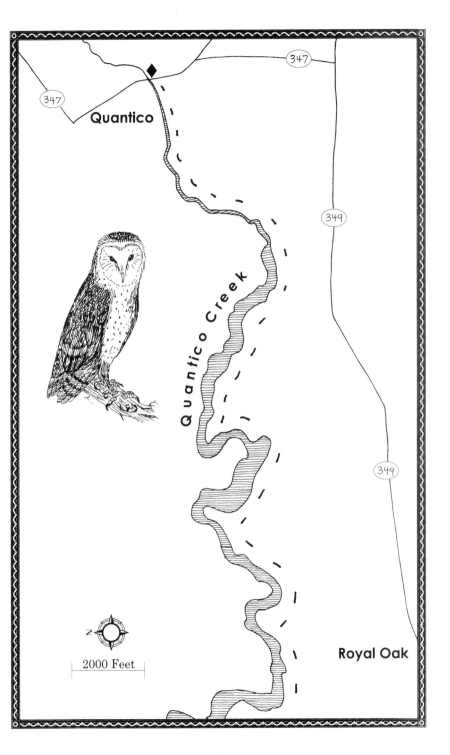

Smith Island

Trip 38

Length: 7 miles circumnavigation, add more to allow for poking around the wildlife refuge next door.

Time: 3½+ hours

Width: Small channels to open water

Difficulties: Wind on open water

Location: In the Chesapeake Bay west of James Island State Park

General description: Smith Island is Maryland's only inhabited offshore island in the Chesapeake Bay. The island resembles a jigsaw puzzle with small creeks fragmenting the pieces. From the water, the paddler views a panorama of marshland and hummocks. Of additional interest are the working crab and oyster boats along the way. Martin National Wildlife Refuge, adjacent to the north, hosts large heron rockeries in the spring and summer and migratory ducks and geese in the fall and winter.

Notes: The island was named for Captain John Smith who visited the island in 1608. Blackbeard, the notorious pirate, also used the island as a layover for his forays on local shipping. Robert E. Lee came to inspect his property (his wife's family possession) as it was the perfect place to pasture livestock - no fences needed! As in Tangier, most residents will maneuver on bicycles or golf carts as the road is only one mile long. Notice the above-ground cemeteries necessitated by the high water table. Locals speak with an Elizabethan accent, not unlike the early days of European activity in American when the Chesapeake Bay was the "highway" for colonial travel.

Access point(s):
♦ Public ramp in Ewell
♦ See "Ferry Information" in back of this book

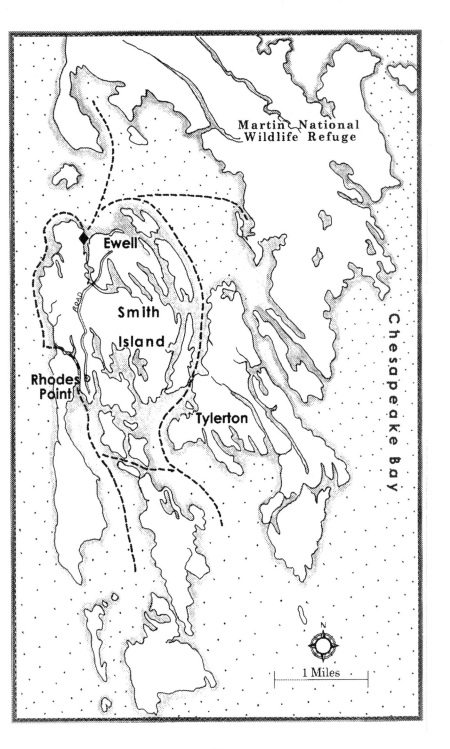

Swan Creek

Trip 39

Length: 4+ miles round trip

Time: 2+ hours

Width: ½ mile at outset tapering to a small sheltered creek

Difficulties: Other sailing boats in area

Location: Rock Hall

General description: Swan Creek is a study in contrasts - new and old, open and wild, neatly sequestered sailboats and genteel civility. The creek begins at Gratitude, named for the old excursion ferry from Baltimore. From that point you are likely to encounter eagles, herons, ospreys and other abundant marshland wildlife.

Notes: In June, this is a prime area to observe cow-nose rays. Rays are unique in appearance. Their body is flat like a pancake with their pectoral fins spread from their sides like "wings." They have no air bladder like fish, so they must keep moving or they will sink. Despite these primitive characteristics, they have been swimming in these waters for hundreds of millions of years. Rays are bottom dwellers, spending most of their time covered with sand with only their eyes protruding, waiting for prey. Other times they may glide along the bottom stirring up the mud and sand in hope of locating food. Although some sources say rays are not edible, it was the main meat substance on the TV hit *Survivor*. The flavor is said to improve if it is bled immediately and soaked in lemon juice or vinegar before cooking. This rids the meat of urea which can give a bitter taste.

Access point(s):
♦ Spring Cove public landing. Take SR 445N, left on Spring Cove Rd., bear right at fork.

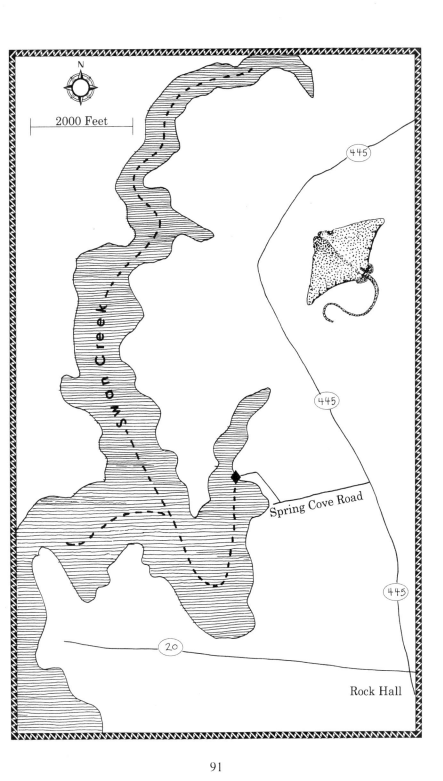

Tangier Island

Trip 40

Length: 10 miles or less

Time: 5 hours or less

Width: Small channels only a few feet wide, larger guts and channels, open waters of the Bay

Difficulties: The passage across the Bay is too dangerous to be attempted. Individual boats may be carried from Crisfield on the mail boat if there is enough room (call 757-891-2240 to check).

Location: In the Bay six miles below the MD-VA State line.

General description: While the beaches and marsh surrounding the island are interesting, the main attraction is the working waterfront community. Paddle among the stilt-supported crab houses where the catch is unloaded and processed. The island claims to be the soft-shelled crab capital of the world. Most residents use golf carts to get about. The cemeteries are above ground. The locals speak "tourist" English to be understood in their shops, but catch a conversation amongst themselves and you will be hard-pressed to understand them. Tangier "English" is similar to old English spoken in Elizabethan times. Have an ice cream at Spanky's, a 50's parlor.

Notes: The island first went to settlers' hands in 1666 when the Indians traded it for two overcoats. From Tangier Island, during the War of 1812, the British fleet plundered Virginia, burned Washington, and embarked to bombard the port of Baltimore. During that fateful battle Francis Scott Key penned the "The Star Spangled Banner" and set his lyrics to a popular English drinking song.

Access point(s):
♦ Only by ferry boat (See information in the back of this book.)

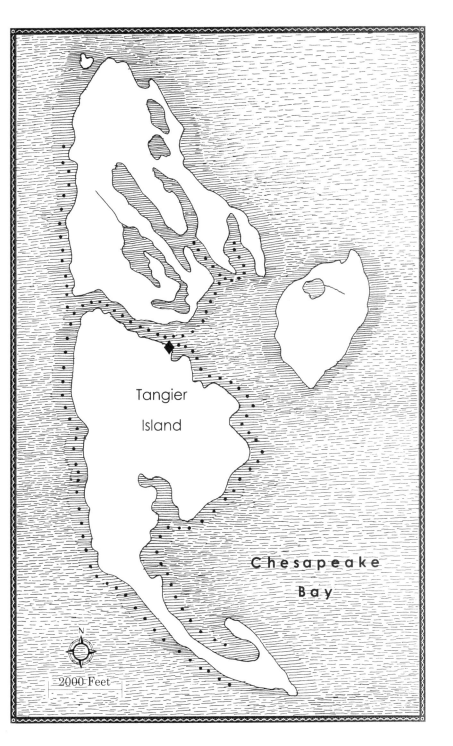

Tavern Creek

Trip 41

Length: 4 miles round trip

Time: 2 hours

Width: ¼ mile

Difficulties: Occasional wind, power and sail boat traffic

Location: Rock Hall

General description: From Rock Hall Beach cross the Bay to the almost hidden entrance to the creek. Tavern Creek is largely undeveloped, with few boats about because of its shallow depths. Abundant wildlife abounds, especially lots of herons fishing the water's edge. Glide over the beds of sub-aquatic vegetation before making the turn for home. There is a very small beach just inside the creek entrance before making the crossing to Rock Hall.

Notes: Beds of aquatic grasses provide food and shelter for a wide variety of crabs, juvenile fish, and wintering waterfowl. Akin to other vegetation, these grasses absorb nutrients like nitrogen and phosphorus, which in excess promote rapid algae growth. This reduces the amount of light reaching the grasses and when they die and decompose, valuable oxygen is also consumed.

Like all green plants, Bay grasses produce oxygen, an important and sometimes scarce commodity in the Chesapeake. Bay grasses also filter and trap suspended sediment which otherwise cloud the water and can bury bottom-dwelling organisms. By reducing wave action, grasses also help keep the shoreline from erosion.

Access point(s):
♦ Rock Hall Beach. Take last paved road on left off SR 20W.

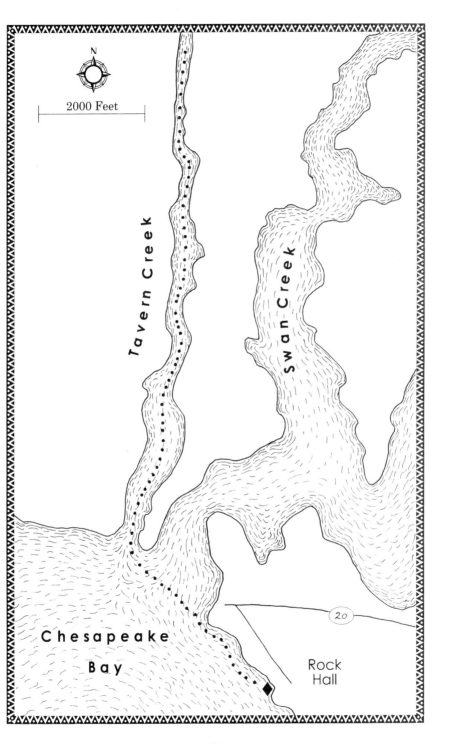

Taylors Island Passage

Trip 42

Length: 7 miles

Time: 3½ hours

Width: 50' - 2500'

Difficulties: The danger of getting lost is real. Use your compass and 7½ USGS topo maps (Taylors Island and Golden Hill). Without maps, one might consider a round trip venture from any one of the access points.

Location: End of SR 16, approximately 10 miles south of Cambridge

General description: Dorchester County has been called the "Everglades of Maryland." Vast marshlands, punctuated by pine growth hummocks, make this one of the finest trips in Maryland. The wildlife is plentiful, especially during migratory seasons. Edward Gertler writes in his book *Maryland and Delaware Canoe Trails*, "Here lies one of the most extensive tracts of unspoiled tidewater canoeing in Maryland."

Notes: A map of waterways presents the navigator with innumerable choices. There is no stream direction so start where you want. Explore a few of the less direct routes; a trip up the side channels will make the venture more interesting. Any course one takes through this wide world of vast marshes and piney hummocks will be engaging.

Access point(s):
- Bridge on SR 16 over Slaughter Creek
- Bridge on Smithville Rd. over Beaverdam Creek
- Bridge on SR 335 over Great Marsh Creek

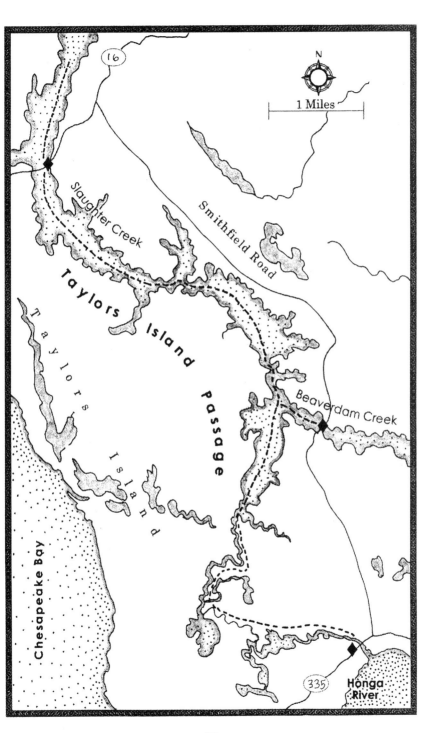

Tilghman Island
Dogwood Harbor

Trip 43

Length: 3 miles round trip

Time: 1½ hours

Width: Open water

Difficulties: Wind

Location: 7 miles west of St. Michaels

General description: Even though one travels beside the marshlands observing the abundant waterfowl, it is likely that the highlight of this trip will be to be among the skipjacks located in Dogwood Harbor.

Notes: During the winter skipjacks, North America's last working sailboat, will be dredging the waters for oysters; the other seasons will find them in safe harbor tied alongside the docks. These boats harken back to the frenzied glory days when the oyster harvest was a highly prized bonanza. Now, over a century later, a few of these magnificent sailing workboats continue the winter dredging tradition.

Oysters are hermaphrodites, beginning life as males and two years later becoming females, laying about 500 million eggs in one year. Oysters filter silt, trash and pollutants from the water. One oyster can cleanse as much as 50 gallons of water on a warm day. Will the endangered oyster recover sufficiently to restore the fleet or are we eye witnesses to the demise of a very special way of life?

Access point(s):
♦ ½ mile past Knapps Narrows Bridge at Dogwood Harbor

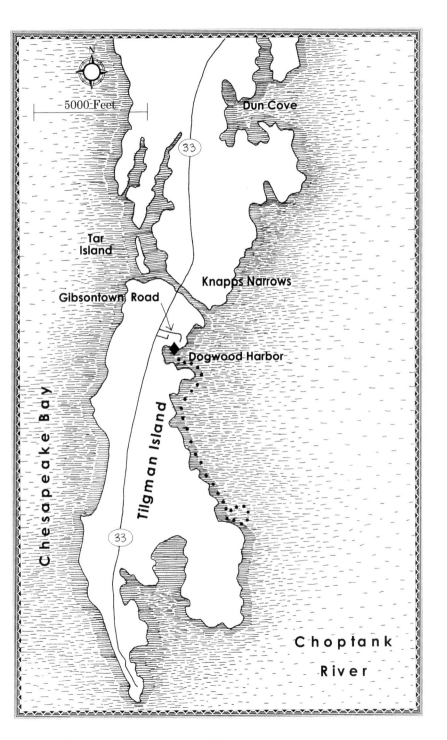

Tilghman Island
Dun Cove

Trip 44

Length: 5 miles round trip

Time: 2½ hours

Width: Open water

Difficulties: Wind

Location: 7 miles west of St. Michaels

General description: Padding to and within Dun Cove places the paddler alongside the vast marshes surrounding the island. A great variety of waterfowl can be viewed here.

Notes: Capt. Dan Vaughan, a master carver whose works have been distributed around the world, has been carving a classic Mid-Atlantic "working style" bird for over 25 years. The common loon and pintail carvings are his hallmark. Loons frequent the Bay, rivers and creeks during their spring and fall migrations. A kayak tour with Dan (phone # 410-886-2083) can be arranged and a close-up view of these birds is just about guaranteed.

Tilghman Island was first charted by Captain John Smith in 1608. Boat building was a natural on the island and two of the most popular types built have been the log canoe and the skipjack, dating from the 1800s. Even today, the dwindling fleet of skipjacks is used for oyster dredging in season and visitors delight in seeing these unique vessels at the dock or under sail.

Access point(s):
♦ ½ mile past Knapps Narrows Bridge at Dogwood Harbor

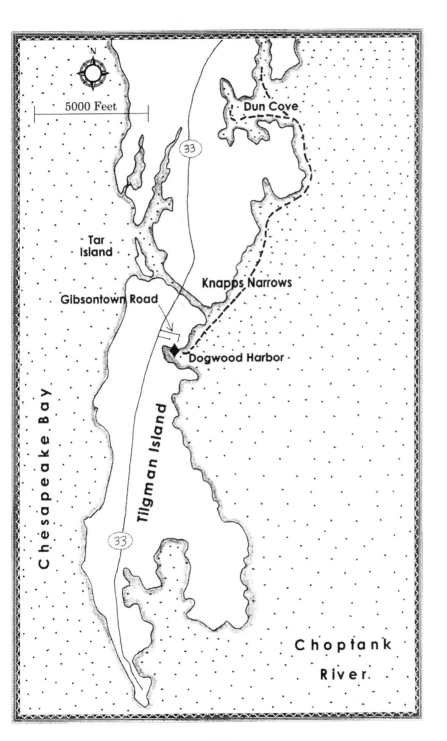

Tilghman Island
Circumnavigate Tar Island

Trip 45

Length: 3 miles round trip

Time: 1½ hours

Width: 100' through the Narrows then into open water

Difficulties: Wind is always a factor in open water.

Location: 13 miles west of St. Michaels

General description: During this circumnavigation of Tar Island you will be over the flats around Tilghman Island. Watch herons and egrets fishing. See terns diving for minnows or a green heron on a piling stretching to reach his dinner. Osprey circle overhead and tend to their young in nests built on many of the channel markers. Bald eagles also grace the skies year round.

Notes: Before taking the trip, educate yourself by stopping by the Chesapeake Bay Maritime Museum at Navy Point in St. Michaels. The museum brings to life the story of the Bay and the people who have lived around it. It contains the world's largest collection of traditional Bay boats. At the docks you will meet *Rosie Parks*, one of the few remaining skipjacks which once harvested hundreds of bushels of oysters every day.

A distinctive house style (circa 1890), which some refer to as the "V" Shape, has three gables on the front and has become a Tilghman Island classic. Many houses of this style were built on the island, but only a few remain.

Access point(s):
♦   ½ mile past Knapps Narrows Bridge at Dogwood Harbor

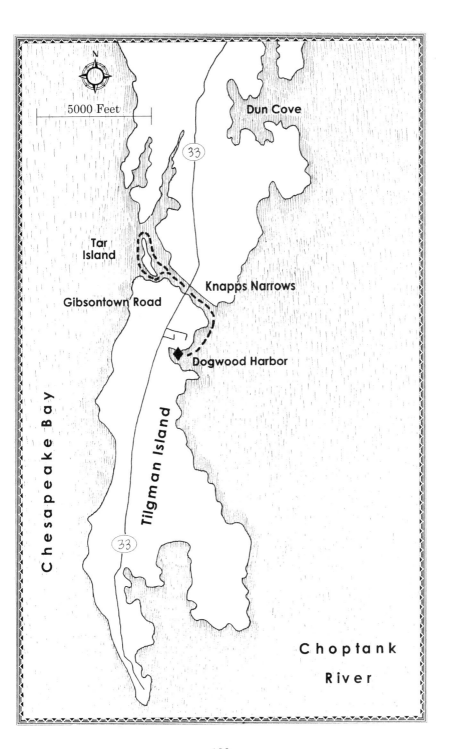

Transquaking River

Trip 46

Length: 12 miles

Time: 6 hours

Width: 100' - 300'

Difficulties: Wind, mosquitoes

Location: 6 - 8 miles northwest of Vienna

General description: Beginning at the forested shoreline at Drawbridge Rd., the landscape transforms into meadows of marsh extending as far as the eye can see. A sublime trip awaits the traveler who dips his paddle into these rarely traveled waters that squirm their way through the grasslands. As relaxing as it is beautiful, don't miss this peaceful venture.

Notes: What is the most deadly animal known to man? You are likely to meet up with it on this trip during the summer months, so be prepared. The pesky mosquito is responsible for more human deaths than any other animal. Mosquitos harassed Caesar's troops and the Spanish conquistadores. Twenty-five thousand of these rascals would weigh only one ounce. They can fly thirty miles an hour and their wings beat 400 - 600 times per second. Only females bite, ingesting two to three times their weight in blood. The males subsist on the nectar from plants. Scientist estimate that only 1 out of 200 mosquitos reach maturity. The rest form the bottom of the food chain for fish, shrimp, and birds.

Access point(s):
◆ Drawbridge Rd.
◆ Bestpitch Ferry Rd.

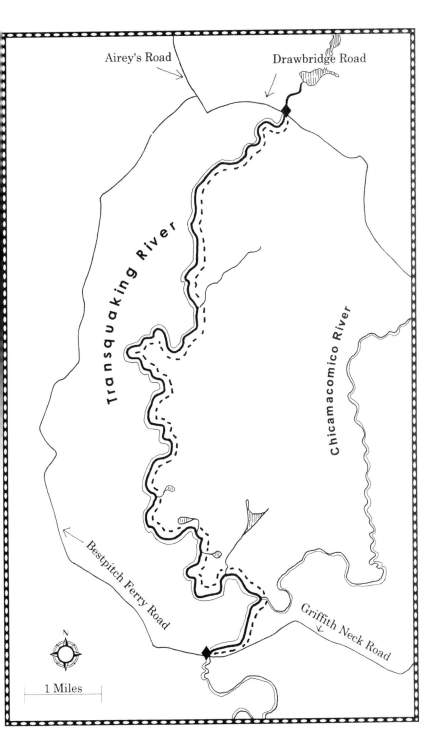

Trap Pond to Raccoon Pond

Trip 47

Length: 3 miles round trip

Time: 1½ hours

Width: 400' within Trap Pond, 5' within canoe trail to Raccoon Pond, 100' within Racoon Pond

Difficulties: None

Location: Laurel

General description: This lush green cruise through beautiful wetland forest surrounded by mysterious swamp, abundant wildlife, wild flowers, and the northernmost stand of natural bald cypress trees in the United States is pure delight. Pursue the constricted canoe trail to Raccoon Pond. Located here are a few cypress trees, but chiefly the freshwater marsh is bordered by pine trees.

Notes: The Pond was created in the early 1800s to power a sawmill during the harvest of bald cypress in the area. Hiking trails surround the pond and birdwatching is popular. The birds inhabiting this area include the great blue heron, owl, hummingbird, bald eagle and the endangered pileated woodpecker. The pileated woodpecker (noted by its crested red head) is the model for "Woody Woodpecker."

Many of the animals and plants here were of great use to the Indians who lived in this part of Sussex county 2000 to 5000 years ago. Plants from the area were employed for baskets, nets, and even medicines. Deer, beaver, rabbits, and waterfowl were valuable sources of food, skins, and raw materials.

Access point(s):
♦ Boat launch at Trap Pond State Park

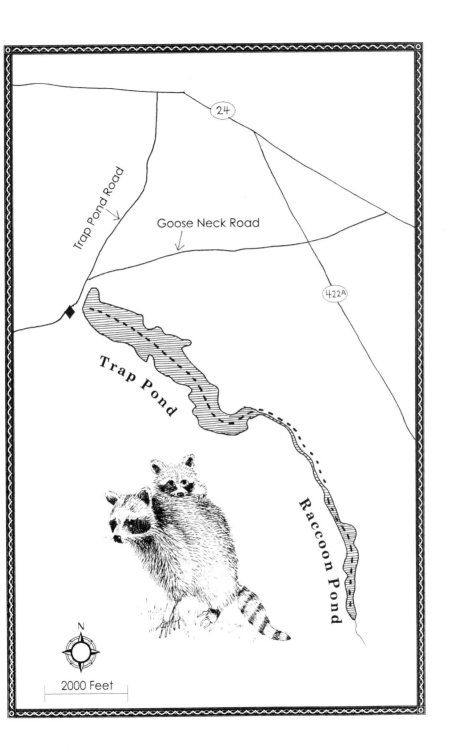

Trussum Pond

Trip 48

Length: 1 mile round trip

Time: Linger

Width: 500'

Difficulties: Summertime duckweed may cover the surface making movement through the water more bothersome. It is sometimes difficult to identify the main channel; however, persistence and a tad of curiosity can lead you up to a mile and a half past the dam.

Location: 1½ miles south of Trap Pond State Park

General description: This incredibly scenic swamp-like pond numbers among the most picturesque in all of Delaware. Graceful green foliage and its extensive collection of bald cypress are a treat for the eyes; some of the cypress measure up to 106 feet in height. Loblolly pines, Spanish oak, and water oak form the outer canopy of vegetation while white cedar, red maple, and American holly constitute the lush, cozy undergrowth. Numerous cypress knees protrude from the lily-clad water, duckweed clothes the surface in the summertime, and draping floral designs adorn the surrounding trees. Paddling through this refreshing beauty is sure to invigorate your day.

Notes: One meaning of the word *loblolly* is "mud puddle," for it is here where the loblolly pine often grows. Other names include "Bull Pine" for its handsome size and "Rosemary Pine" for its fragrance. The American Holly has whitish fine-textured wood especially useful in cabinet inlays, handles, carvings, and rulers. Many kinds of birds and animals eat the bitter berries.

Access point(s):
♦ 2.6 miles southwest of SR 24 on Trap Pond Rd.

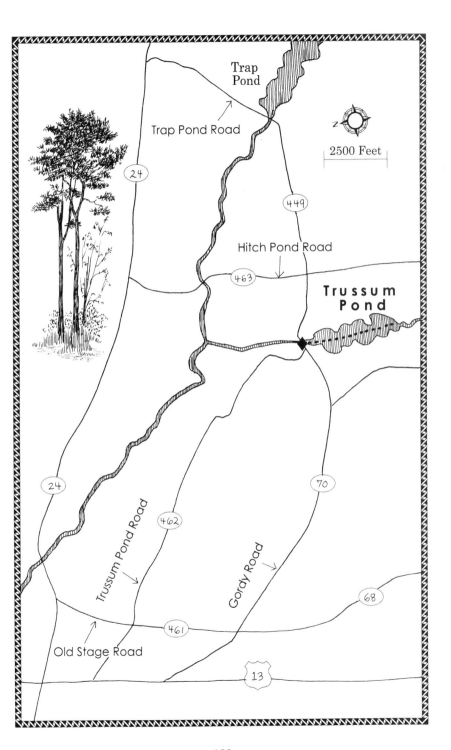

Tuckahoe Creek

Trip 49

Length: 5½ miles one-way only due to the strong current.

Time: 2½ hours

Width: 15' - 90'

Difficulties: None

Location: Tuckahoe State Park

General description: A beautiful, narrow run through a small, snarled swamp and deep, dense forest. If you are looking for secluded beauty, this is the place. Bald eagles, ospreys and great blue herons are commonly seen. Beavers and muskrats might swim by your craft. The brisk current contributes to making this a relaxing and most enjoyable passage. Add this to your "must do" list.

Notes: The beaver is a very large rodent, as long as 46" and usually weighing from 45 - 60 lbs. As an alarm signal, it uses its large flat tail to slap the water. Beavers living along lakes generally make their homes in lodges, mounds of gnawed sticks piled up to 6' high along the banks. Those living along streams such as the Tuckahoe generally make burrows in the banks with an underwater entrance. To fell a tree, the beaver gnaws a deep groove around it. Normally trees 5" - 6" are selected and can be felled in 3 minutes. However, you may see where beavers have attempted to take down a tree even 30" in diameter. It either eats the bark on site or stores the tree for winter by poking the end into the soft mud beneath the water. The beaver is nocturnal and most likely to be observed in the evening.

Access point(s):
♦ Launch ramp on Main St. in Hillsboro (SR 404)
♦ Bridge below dam on Crouse Mill Rd. at Tuckahoe St. Pk.

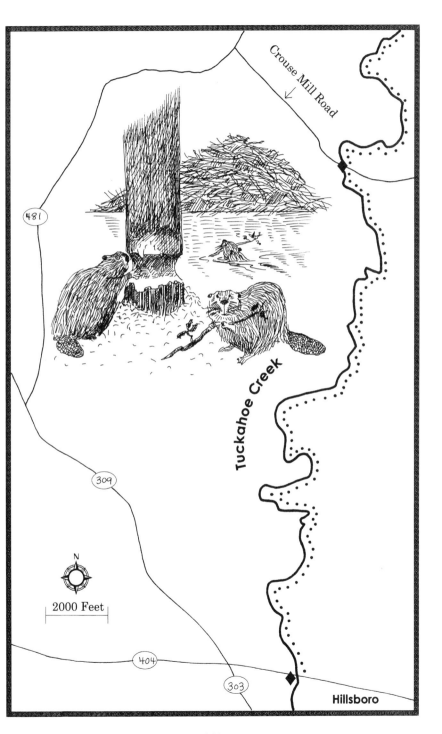

Wye Island Natural Management Area

Trip 50

Length: 14 miles (circumnavigation)

Time: 7 hours

Width: Varies greatly from 300' to open water.

Difficulties: Wind, although one can usually find protection on windy days on the lee side of land.

Location: 10 miles northwest of Easton

General description: The shore of the island is forested; however, the opposite shore is mostly developed. In season the migratory waterfowl of many varieties are bounteous. Canada geese are nearly always present in varying numbers depending on the season.

Notes: facts about the Canada goose (life applications here?)
As each goose flaps its wings it creates an "uplift" for the birds that follow. By flying in a "V" formation, the whole flock adds 71% greater flying range than if each bird flew alone. When the lead goose tires, it rotates back into the formation and another goose flies to the point position. The geese flying in formation honk to encourage those up front to keep up their speed. When a goose gets sick, wounded or shot, two geese drop out of formation and follow it down. They stay with it until it dies or is able to fly again. Then, they launch out with another formation or catch up with the flock. - *Outward Bound*

On route to Wye Island on SR 662 you will pass the largest white oak (see historical marker) in the United States.

Access point(s):
♦   End of Wye Landing Lane

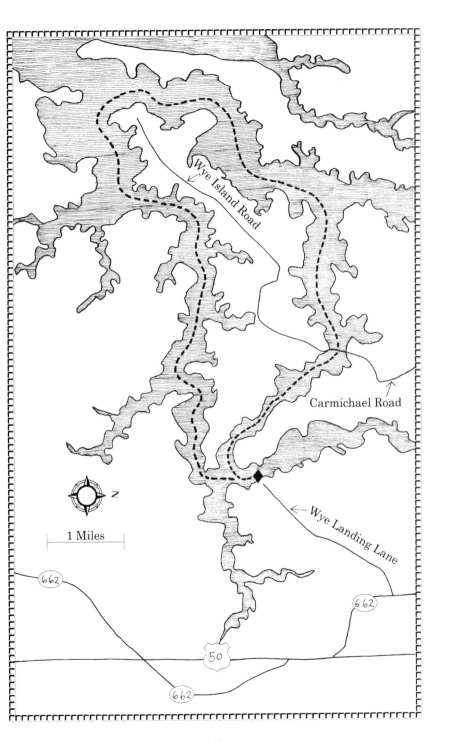

" Surely there is something
in the unruffled calm of nature that
overawes our little anxieties and doubts;
the sight of the deep blue sky, and the
clustering stars above, seem to
impart a quiet to the mind."
— Jonathan Edwards

Waters On or Flowing into the Atlantic Ocean

©Photo by Ed White

Appoquinimink River

Trip 51

Length: 8+ miles round trip

Time: 4+ hours

Width: 60' - 300'

Difficulties: The tidal current at Odessa is very strong so consider your route and launch on the appropriate tide. To ensure adequate depth, the upper areas are best traveled at high tide.

Location: Odessa, 25 miles south of Wilmington

General description: This is the northwest most scenic creek in Delaware. Much of this stream meanders through tidal marsh, with woodlands beyond, passing through several ponds or lakes. From the launch point, the passage upstream winds through an intriguing, narrow, convoluted waterway. Downstream takes the paddler through high reeds in the open marsh.

Notes: Settled in 1721, Odessa was once known as Cantrell's Bridge. In 1855 the city fathers told the railroad to lay their track elsewhere as the city was content with its prosperity from their grain-shipping industry. The name Odessa came from the Russian grain port on the Black Sea.

Before the Civil War, Odessa was an important station on the Underground Railroad. Many 18th and 19th century homes are in the area.

Access point(s):
◆ SR 299 in Odessa, ½ mile east of town center

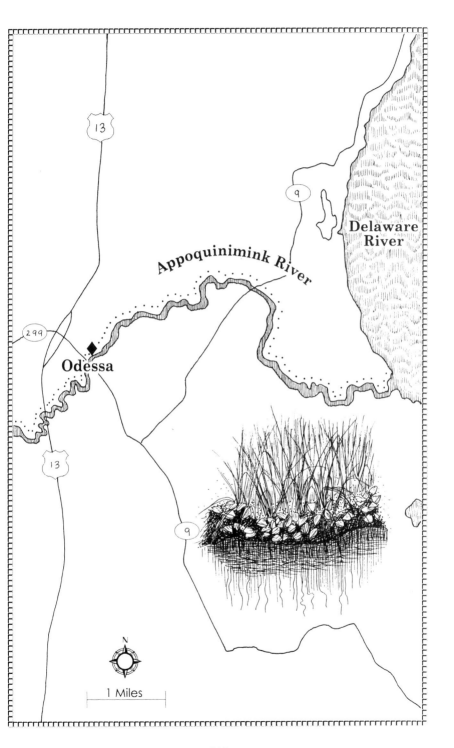

Assateague State Park and National Seashore

Trip 52

Length: 13 miles one way or a round trip of varying distances from the Assateague launch site (Ferry Landing)
- 4 miles round trip to Tingles Island
- 10 miles round trip to Pine Tree
- 14 miles round trip to James Gut

Time: 6½ hours

Width: Open water, also protected waters of smaller channels

Difficulties: Shallow water and wind can be a problem, lots of bugs during the summer.

Location: Barrier island of Maryland and Virginia

General description: Vast marshes, hummocks, coves, and guts cover the entire route. Take advantage of beachheads in the marsh to meander across this thirty-five miles long but narrow island and beachcomb on the ocean. The park's numbered canoe/kayak trail helps to locate where you are, but a good map and compass are also a big help. Campsites are identifiable from the water by signage. There is no camping on the Virginia side.

Notes: The famous wild ponies roam the island and are easily seen. Be careful and do not attempt to closely approach. It is thought their ancestors were stranded from the wreck of galleons centuries ago. Vast numbers of waterfowl pass through here during the migratory season. From April through summer, thousands of herons, egrets, and terns fish the shallow waters of the Bay.

Access point(s):
- ♦ Old Ferry Landing Rd. in Assateague National Seashore
- ♦ Tom's Cove in Chincoteague State Park

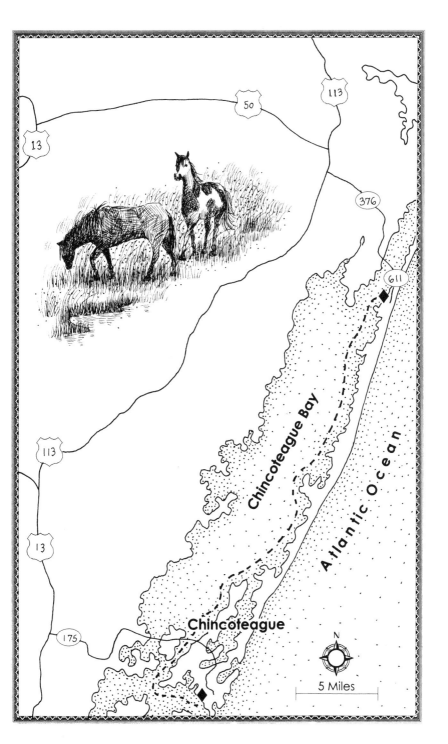

Blackbird Creek

Trip 53

Length: 8 miles

Time: 4 hours

Width: 60' - 500'

Difficulties: This is a tidal river so consider paddling with the current.

Location: Approximately 10 miles north of Smyrna

General description: A lovely winding path to seaward takes one through marshlands bordered by the high reeds of saltwater cordgrass. Above Blackbird Landing, intimacy with the creek increases as it meanders through the swamp lands passing through a mixture of hardwood and softwood forest. Enjoy!

Notes: Black duck, mallard, and wood duck are the most common nesting birds on this waterway. The wood duck is one of the most beautiful birds and considered the tastiest of all ducks. This colorful bird often perches in trees. In flight, the white belly contrasts with the dark body and wings. Additionally, during the spring and fall migrations, ducks and geese of many varieties alight on these waters.

Herons, egrets, ibis, hawks, osprey and bald eagles can also be seen. Numerous muskrats reside in the brackish and saltwater wetlands, together with beaver and otter in lesser numbers. Unfortunately, posted signs warn of eating fish taken from this stream.

Access point(s):
- Blackbird Landing on Blackbird Landing Rd. (access difficult but possible)
- Stave Landing Rd., landing is 1.2 miles from SR 9

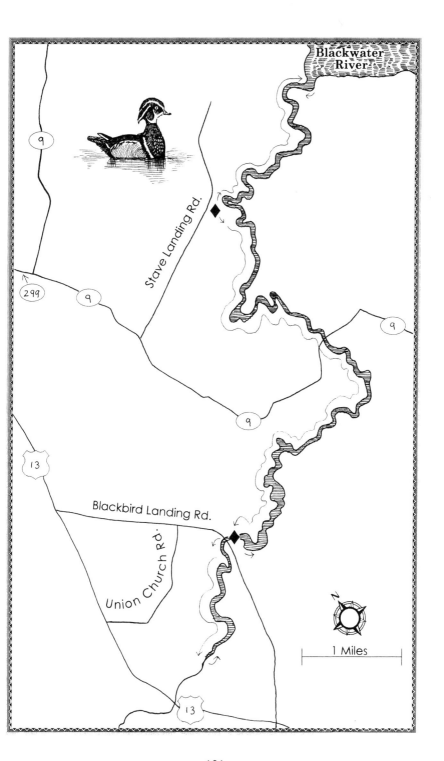

Broadkill River

Trip 54

Length: 10 miles

Time: 5 hours

Width: 100' - 300'

Difficulties: None

Location: Comprises a portion of the outer boundary of Prime Hook National Wildlife Refuge northwest of Cape Henlopen.

General description: If launching at Milton, the early parts of this trip pass through partly forested, swampy shores. As the river progresses, one sees less woods and the extension of increasingly wider marsh borders until one is eventually within the ocean of marsh nearing Oyster.

Notes: Nearby Cape Henlopen and Beach Plum Island are particularly recommended as the most productive places for viewing a large variety of shorebirds. The Delaware Bay and its shores are the second largest stop in the western hemisphere for northbound shorebirds. Unlike other birds who stop frequently to refuel along their migratory route, shorebirds are unique. Instead of feeding frequently along the way, shorebirds make only a couple of stops at "staging areas," and therefore must have plenty of food available at the precise time they arrive. In the fall, concentrations of Canada geese, snow geese, black ducks, mallards, pintails, teal, and wood ducks are of particular interest, many of whom migrate through the area.

Access point(s):
- Mulberry Street beside fishing pier in Milton
- Oyster Rocks Rd., SR 264

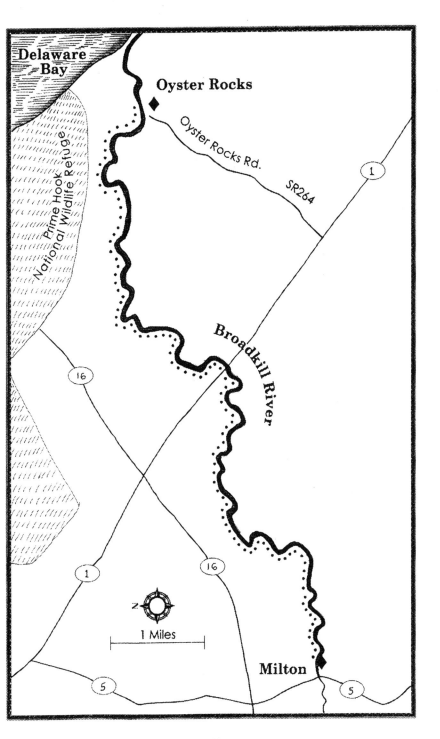

Cape Henlopen

Trip 55

Length: 6 miles round trip

Time: 3 hours

Width: Open water

Difficulties: The trip around the cape is too difficult for any but the most experienced. Currents, waves, and rips are just too strong.

Location: Lewes

General description: Paddle northwest along the sand dunes. This is a lovely stretch of beach and the rocking of the waves plus the serenity of the large expanse of open dunes will assure a most enjoyable trip.

Notes: Ninety-seven percent of the shorebirds that stop over in the Delaware Bay are "sandpipers." Four species comprise this group: the Red Knot, Sanderling, Ruddy Turnstone, and Semipalmated Plover. The Red Knot has a robin-red head and under parts with yellow-green legs. Sanderlings are bright rusty-red above and on their breast. They can be seen running behind receding waves probing for food. The Ruddy Turnstone has a pattern of black, white and rust-red on top. It uses its bill to flip stones and shells in search for food. The Semipalmated (means half web-footed) Plover is dark brown above, white below with a single dark band around its neck like a collar. It runs with its head up, dabbing suddenly for food. North of Roosevelt Inlet is the partially sunken wreck of a wooden steamship. Red Knobs and Ruddy Turnstones are likely to be found atop this wreck.

Access point(s):
♦ Cape Henlopen State Park next to fishing pier

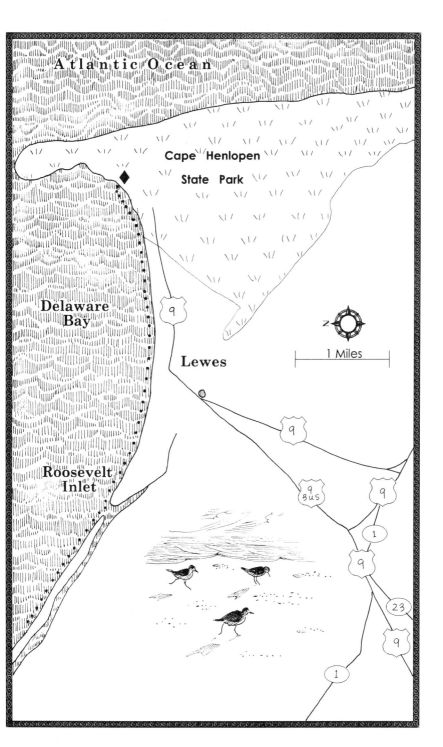

Indian River Bay

Trip 56

Length: 4 miles or more

Time: 2 hours or take longer

Width: Open water on Indian River Bay and/or much narrower and more protected waters on the adjoining creeks

Difficulties: Wind on the open water

Location: Holts Landing State Park

General description: Wander through the saltwater marshes and you will be immersed in the abundant wildlife of the Bay, including the ever present seagulls, egrets and herons above, and crabs beneath the surface. Learn about these gifts to us and enjoy a delightful outing.

Notes: Holts Landing State Park conducts tours in this area going among Vines Creek, Pepper Creek, and Blackwater Creek. Call (302) 539-9060 for information and reservations.

The Horseshoe Crab is an amazing animal. It is often called a living fossil for it is one of earth's oldest creatures, having survived successfully in the sea for over 600 million years. Interestingly, it is not a true crab, but rather in a class by itself most closely related to spiders. It appears quite intimidating, but is really harmless and can be picked up and examined without danger. It looks like a flattened helmet on the outside, while the underside has five pairs of walking legs. As it walks, the spines on the upper part of the legs grind its food, much like teeth. In fact, this crab is unable to eat except when walking.

Access point(s):
♦ Boat launch within Holts Landing State Park

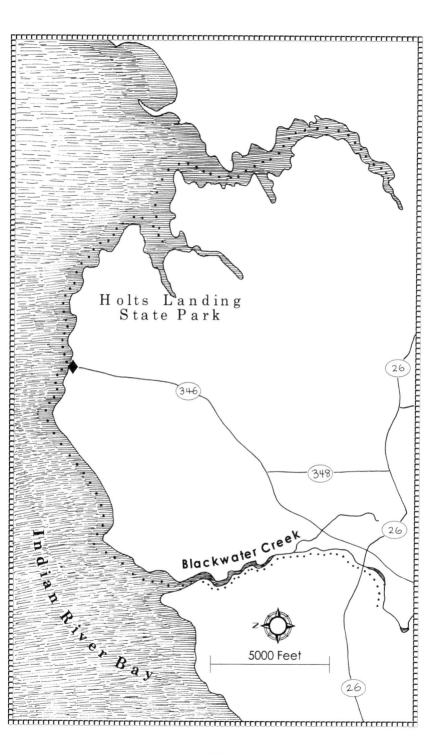

Leipsic River

Trip 57

Length: 5 miles or longer if going to Bombay Hook

Time: 2½+ hours

Width: 25' - 50', wider nearer Bombay Hook

Difficulties: None

Location: Leipsic, 3 miles south of Smyrna

General description: Beginning at Lake Garrison, one immediately encounters a vast array of lush greenery. This beautiful forest quietly changes into expansive marsh grass as the current comfortably sweeps the paddler downstream.

Notes: The paddler may wish to continue downriver through the beautiful marshes of Bombay Hook National Wildlife Refuge, a maze of creeks all appealing for investigation. The Bombay Hook area nurtures large numbers of Canada geese and other waterfowl making the Refuge a worthwhile addition. Beginning in September through early March, this refuge is one of the best places in the area to see (and hear) thousands of snow geese. At sunset, they keep coming and coming, until the ponds look like they're covered with snow. Be aware that there is no access in the Refuge, requiring one to return to Front Street in Leipsic. In summer, the shore birds are impressive; several varieties of egrets and herons, and hundreds of glossy ibises can be seen. Marsh wrens, indigo buntings, avocets, baby foxes, marsh hawks, and lots of little crabs can be viewed.

Access point(s):
♦ Garrison Lake fishing area off US 13 approximately 4 miles south of Smyrna
♦ Front Street in Leipsic

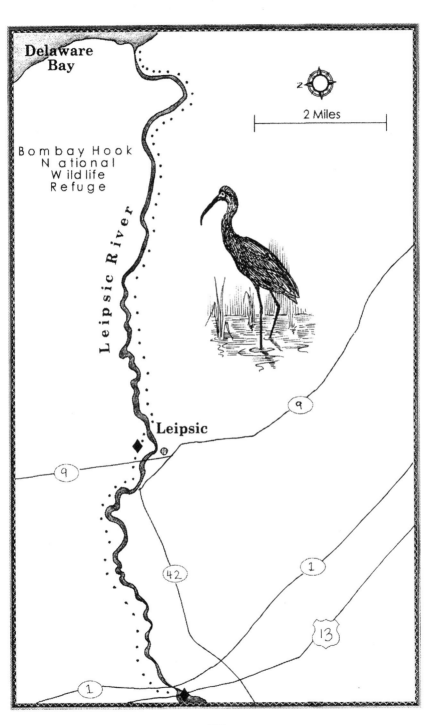

Little Assawoman Bay

Trip 58

Length: Approximately 5 miles

Time: 2½ hours

Width: Open water; sloughs, guts, and channels will be more sheltered.

Difficulties: None. Occasionally the wind picks up.

Location: West of Fenwick Island State Park

General description: Saltwater marsh forms the fringes of the Bay. Within its grasses, birdwatchers may identify many species of waterfowl. Osprey, herons and perhaps a bald eagle may be spied looking for a meal. Expect the ever present gulls and terns in the summer months.

Notes: Fenwick Island State Park, the eastern edge of Little Assawoman Bay, was reinforced as part of the Delaware coastal defense system. A concrete observation tower, manned during the war to scout for both U-boats and a surface invasion fleet, still stands near the northern boundary as a testament to more perilous times.

Little Assawoman Bay is a popular place to catch Blue Crabs. Each female Blue Crab deposits over one million eggs to the swimmerets on the underside of her abdomen. Only one out of one million eggs will reach adulthood. A young crab grows quickly during the summer, molting every 3 to 5 days and increasing up to ⅓ its size with each molt, molting 18 - 23 times before reaching adult size.

Access point(s):
- ◆ Sassafras Landing at the end of Double Bridge Rd.
- ◆ Mulberry Landing at the end of Camp Barnes Rd.

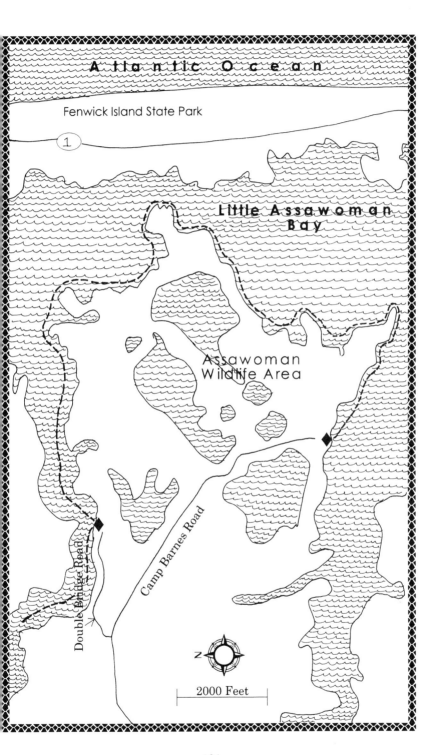

Murderkill River

Trip 59

Length: 7½ miles from Killen Pond to Frederica

Time: 4 hours

Width: 15' - 40' (wider at Coursey Pond)

Difficulties: Avoid spillways at Killen Pond and at Coursey Pond.

Location: Frederica

General description: An appealing run through marsh and forests into Coursey Pond; thereafter, the forest view dominates until nearing Frederica where the marsh takes over.

Notes: Consider paddling Killen Pond upstream from SR 384. The beauty of the pond will prove to be worth your additional time and considerable effort. Also consider going south at Carpenter's Bridge through Big Cripple Swamp on Brown's Branch for additional extended pleasure.

The brutal name of this waterway derives from a massacre of early Dutch settlers by the Indians, or vice versa, depending on whom you ask. Why the gruesome theme to so many of these rivers and creeks: Broadkill, Murderkill, Slaughter and Killen Pond? One explanation: the surrounding land was settled by the Dutch and in their native tongue the word for river or creek is "kill." Hopefully these gruesome names have been born from a mere translation glitch.

Access point(s):
- Chimney Hill Rd. to launch at Killen Pond State Park. Follow signs to State Park from SR 12.
- SR 12 at Frederica
- SR 15

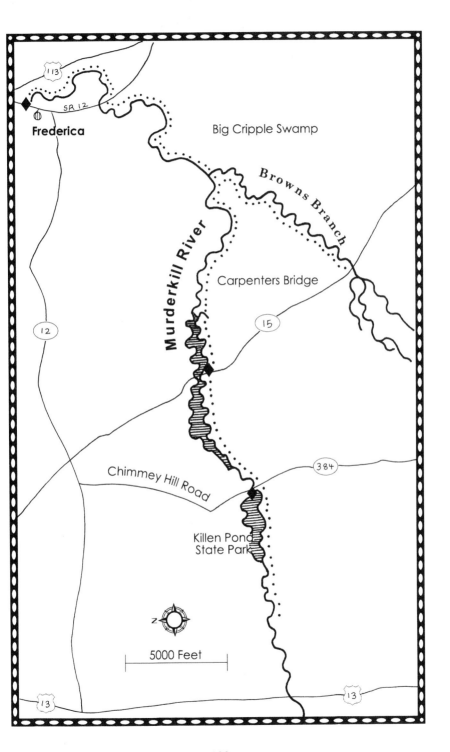

Old Mill Creek

Trip 60

Length: 6 miles

Time: 3 hours

Width: 20' - 100'

Difficulties: The launch at SR 1 could be a little shallow at low tide, but it is worth the carrying that might be required.

Location: 2 miles northwest of Lewes

General description: This is one beautiful creek, not to be missed! Initially passing through a very narrow corridor, the upper portion travels through hardwoods dominated by red maples. Soon marsh appears with small islands of cedar trees. The downstream trip opens into the breathtaking spectacle of wide open marshlands. The trip upstream from Oyster Rocks on the Broadkill River may require a more strenuous effort, but it can be done..

Notes: In the fall, red maples are emblazoned with color. The pioneers made ink and cinnamon-brown and black dye from the bark. Henry David Thoreau wrote of the maple: *"How beautiful, when a whole tree is like one great scarlet fruit full of ripe juices, every leaf, from lowest limb to topmost spire, all aglow, especially if you look toward the sun! What more remarkable object can there be in the landscape?"*

Even today, cedar logs long immersed in the swamp are well preserved and are still suitable for lumber. Pioneers prized the durable wood for log cabins, especially floors and shingles.

Access point(s):
♦ Behind red barn on SR 1 near Red Mill Pond
♦ Oyster Rocks, SR 264

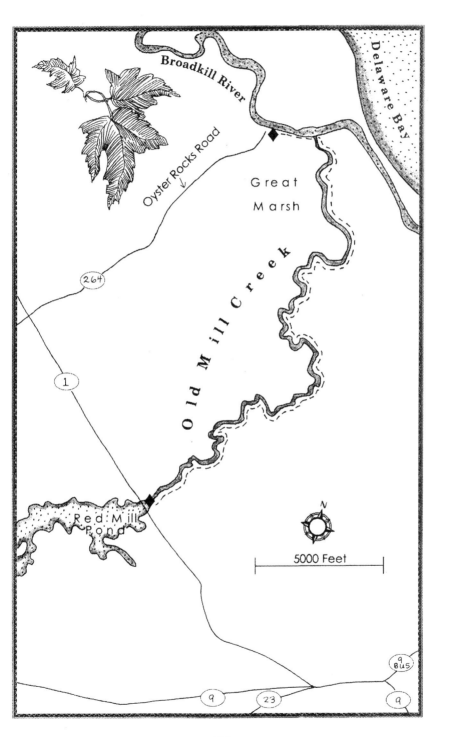

Prime Hook Creek

Trip 61

Length: 7 miles

Time: 3½ hours

Width: 10' - 800'

Difficulties: None

Location: Prime Hook National Wildlife Refuge

General Description: Edward Gertler writes, "This is one of the nicest canoe streams in Delaware." The beginning of this trip near SR 1 leads through several ponds. Gradually a smaller, more personal stream appears bringing you through a swamp forest, then through a wooded corridor beyond which lies a vast marsh. This last section bisects the Prime Hook National Wildlife Refuge and eventually arrives at the Refuge Headquarters.

Notes: As this route is within the Great Atlantic Flyway, it is a strategic place to view the tens of thousands of migratory waterfowl. Along the way in the summer you will be rewarded with patches of floating gardens of water lilies. Muskrats love this plant!

Muskrats construct their homes, similar to beaver lodges, within the marsh. Along the banks, look for raised mounds of aquatic vegetation, especially cattails. These mounds may be 8' in diameter and 5' high. Muskrats also construct feeding platforms distinguished by uneaten grass and reed cuttings. Scat is generally ½" long on banks, logs in or next to the water, and on feeding platforms.

Access point(s):
♦ SR 1 at the campground behind Waples Pond
♦ Refuge HQ. SR 16, left on Turkle Pond Rd.

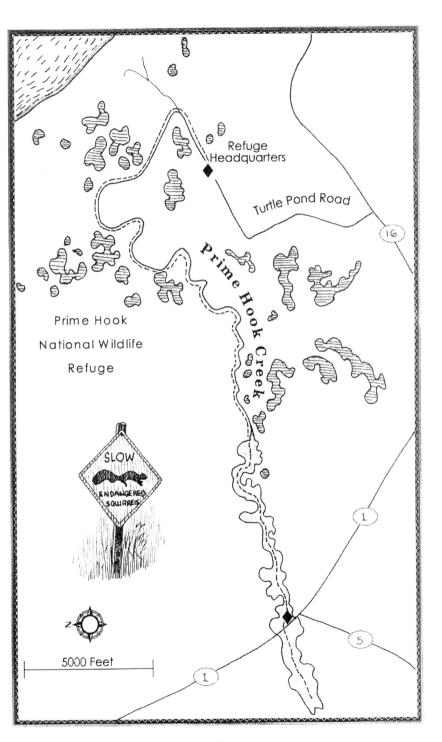

Rehoboth Bay

Trip 62

Length: 4 miles or more round trip

Time: 2+ hours

Width: Open water

Difficulties: Wind on open water

Location: Delaware Seashore State Park

General description: Explore the marshes bordering the creeks up and down the bay side or simply enjoy the long expanse of sand. Stop for a while and rake for clams or float among the colorful windsurfers as they whisk by on a breezy day.

Notes: Clams are commonly found in the Bay. Taking a clam rake, wade in the shallows and scrape the bottom until you hear a "clunk." That sound will usually yield one of the sea's most delicious morsels. The thick shell is easily recognized - whitish to tan on the outside with fine, concentric, heavy rings. With its strong foot, the clam burrows into the mud or sand and extends a siphon tube to draw in the microorganisms in the water. In doing so, it acts as a superb filtering agent for our inland waters.

The clam was used extensively by the Native Americans. The meat provided ample food and the shells were used for tools and ornaments. Beads were made from the shells which when strung together were used like money for trade. The purple portion of the shell was two to four times more valuable than the whiter portions.

Access point(s):
♦ On the beach at the Towers Road bay side exit at the north end of the State Park

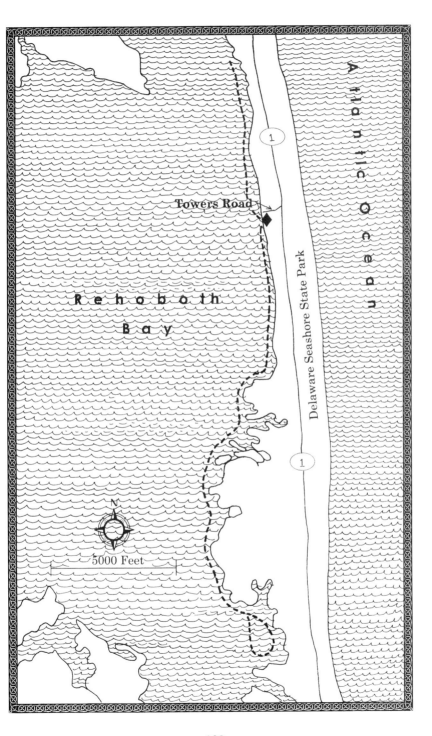

Slaughter Creek

Trip 63

Length: 7 miles

Time: 3½ hours

Width: 50' - 70'

Difficulties: Usually none, maybe a few carries

Location: Prime Hook National Wildlife Refuge

General description: As this creek begins, it flows as a narrow path weaving its way through freshwater marsh bordered by the twisted forests of pine and cedar. The environment begins to change as it continues to flow through vast, unspoiled salt marshes backed by a curtain of forest. In the concluding portion of the journey, the marsh changes from the flats of a salt marsh to a wilder, thicker, more untamed version. Such environments are intriguing as one examines the alteration of these outdoor neighborhoods.

Notes: During the fall and winter, various migratory waterfowl nest here making it an excellent place for viewing our feathered friends. The dense vegetation includes many persimmon trees which make an excellent snack (the flavor is similar to dates) if tasted in the right season, usually after the first frost. If eaten before it ripens, the fruit is *terribly* sour! Persimmons are also gathered to make puddings, cakes and beverages. Opossums, raccoons, skunks, deer and birds also feed upon this fruit. In the "old days" golf club heads were made from persimmon wood. The genus name for "persimmon" means "fruit of the god Zeus."

Access point(s):
♦ Fowler Beach Rd.
♦ 1¼ mile down Cedar Creek at the public boat ramp

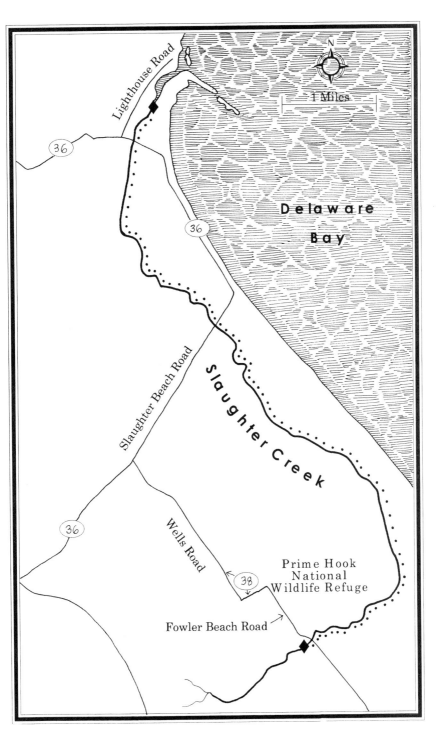

Outfitters

The following outfitters are provided for your reference. Some will be helpful in providing local knowledge, tours, rentals, or shuttle service if you desire. They were selected from a web search of the region. My apologies to those who have been inadvertently omitted.

Delaware

Wilmington
Goldberg 1 the Great OutdoorStore
3626 Kirkwood Highway 19808
(302) 999-0124

Wilderness Canoe Trips
2111 Concord Pike 19803
(302) 653-2227

Maryland

Annapolis
Chesapeake Light Craft
1805 George Avenue 21401
(301) 858-3665 or (410) 267-0137

Springriver Corporation
311 3rd Street 21403
(410) 263-2303

Craft Works Marine Woodworking
Electra Ghost Canoes
7043 Bembe Beach Road 21403
(410) 268-1808

Baltimore
Kayak Tours
710 East Fort Avenue 21230
(410) 576-0774

Springriver Corporation
6434 Baltimore National # P 21228
(410) 788-3377

Cabin John
Potomac Outdoors Limited
7687 Macarthur Boulevard 20818
(301) 320-1544

Camp Outer Quest
7945 Macarthur Boulevard 20818
(301) 229-2860

College Park
Recreational Equipment, Inc.
9801 Rhode Island Ave. 20740
(301) 982-9681

Denton
Talbot Fun and Fitness
206 Market Street 21629
(410) 770-3175

Easton
Easton Cycle and Sport
723 Goldsborough Street 21601
(410) 822-7433

Talbot Fun and Fitness
417 East Dover Street 21601
(410) 820-8995

Havre de Grace
Starrk Moon Kayaks
500 Warren Street 21078
(410) 939-9500
(877) KAY-AKS1 (toll-free)

Germantown
Camp Outerquest
(301) 258-1914

Hagerstown
Bergers Marine Sales
21843 Millers Church Road 21742
(301) 790-3511

Antietam Recreation
9745 Garis Shop Road 21740
(301) 797-7999

Hopewell
Tangier Sound Outfitters
27582 Farm Market Rd. 21838
(410) 968-1803

Knoxville
Cross Country Ski Tours
(301) 695-5177

River and Trail Outfitters
North Harpers Ferry Road 21758
(301) 834-9950 or (301) 695-5177

Ocean City
Ocean City Kayak Company
Shantytown Village 21842
(410) 213-2818

Potomac
Outerquest, Inc.
(301) 299-8825

Rock Hall
Chesapeake Rowing
7280 Swan Creek Road 21661
(410) 639-7172

Chester River Kayak Adventures
5758 Main Street 21661
(410) 639-2001

Rockville
Canoes by Springriver
5606 Randolph Road 20852
(301) 881-5694

Viking Paddles Corporation
112 Frederick Avenue Suite L
20850
(301) 838-3090

Saint Michaels
Tidewater Canvas
1114 South Talbot Street 21663
(410) 745-2468

Salisbury
Survival Products
1116 North Salisbury Blvd. 21801
(410) 543-1244

Smith Island
Ewell Tide Inn
Ewell
(888) 699-2141

Snow Hill
Pocomoke River Canoe Company
312 North Washington St. 21863
(410) 632-3971

Sparks Glencoe
Water Dogs Kayaking Instruction
(410) 329-3688

Tilghman Island
Island Kayak
P.O. Box 357 21671
(410) 886-2083

Vienna
Appalachian Outfitters
Canoe and Kayak Center
2938 Chain Bridge Road 22124
(703) 281-4324

New Jersey
Cape May
Cape May Water Sports
1286 Wilson Drive 08204
(609) 884-8646

Aqua Trails Kayak Tours & Sales
956 Ocean Drive 08204
(609) 884-5600

Miss Chris Marina Kayak Rental
3rd Ave. And Wilson 08204
(609) 884-3351

Cherry Hill
1 Goldberg the Great Outdoor Store
1629Kings Highway North 08002
(856) 795-2244

Newfield
Al & Sams Canoe and Boat Rentals
2626 Weymouth Road 08344
(856) 692-8440

Haddonfield
Cedar River Supply CO
(856) 795-9898

Marlton
Ocean Pines Outdoor Recreation
Education
(856) 985-9775

Vincentown
Adams Canoe Rental
1005 Atsion Road 08088
(609) 268-0189

Vorhees
Goldberg 1 the Great Outdoor
Store
79 State Highway No 73 08043
(856) 753-9800

Wildwood
Schuylkill Outfitters
501 Ocean Avenue 08260
(609) 522-6568

Pennsylvania
Annville
Union Canal Canoe Rental
Blackbridge Road 17003
(717) 838-9580

Bryn Mawr
Schuylkill
1038 West Lancaster Ave. 19010
(610) 520-0970

Camp Hill
Wildware Outfitters
Camp Hill Shopping Mill 17011
(717) 737-2728

Coatsville
Brandywine Outfitters
2096 Strasburg Road 19320
(610) 486-6141

Conshohocken
REI
200 West Ridge Pike 19428
(610) 940-0808

Dallastown
Ullers Ski and Board Shop
2799 South Queen Street 17313
(717) 747-0095

Delta
Starrk Moon Kayaks
497 Cold Cabin Road 17314
(717) 456-7720
(877) 529-2571 (toll-free)

Exton
Goldberg 1 Family Outfitters
Whiteland Town Center 19341
(610) 363-9300

Gilbertsville
Woodstrip Watercraft CO
1818 Swamp Pike 19525
(610) 326-9282

Kellys Nursery Christmas Shoppe
1348 Grosser Road 19525
(610) 369-1778

Marysville
Blue Mountain Outfitters
103 South State Road 17053
(717) 957-2413

Mechanicsville
Canoe Club of Greater Harrisburg
(717) 796-7055

Springfield
Goldberg 1 the Great Outdoor Store
149 Baltimore Pike 19064
(610) 543-1900

Ronks
Leacock Coleman Center
89 Old Leacock Rd. 17572
(717) 768-7174

Warminster
Goldberg 1 the Great Outdoor Store
860 West Street Road 18974
(215) 957-1500

Wrightsville
Shanks Mare Outfitters
2092 Long Level Road 17368
(717) 252-1616

Virginia

Alexandria
Atlantic Canoe and Kayak Co.
1201 North Royal Street 22314
(703) 838-9072 or (703) 780-0066

Arlington
Ski Chalet
2704 Columbia Pike 22204
(703) 521-1700

Aylett
Mattaponi Canoe and Kayaks
11002 West River Road 23009
(804) 769-1449

Falls Church
Recreational Equipment Inc.
3509 Carlin Springs Road 22041
(703) 379-9400

Springriver Corporation
2757 Summerfield Road 22042
(703) 241-2818

Fredericksburg
Clore Brothers Outfitters
5927 River Road 22407
(540) 786-7749

Outdoor Adventures
4721 Plank Road 22407
(540) 786-3334

Rappahannock Outdoors
3219 Fall Hill Avenue 22401
(540) 371-5085

Purcellville
Short Hill Canoe
(540) 668-7159

Vienna
Ski Chalet
8338 Leesburg Pike 22182
(703) 761-3040

Special Thanks to Those Who Helped Along the Way

My family helped tremendously. The front cover indicates that my youngest high school son, Matthew, assisted in this book. He was my companion on the trips - helping with hauling the boat, tenting and cooking along the way. He has even made written contributions that are printed herein. I was blessed by his company. I hope he will continue to grow in his love for the water, yet another facet of God's masterful creation.

My wife, Susan, and oldest son, Heath, were my grammarians, painstakingly reviewing this document. Even though I thought I caught all the errors, they found many that I missed and offered even better ways to communicate the beauty of these waterways more effectively. My sincere gratitude is offered for their work.

My daughter, Ashleigh, while not contributing directly to this work is, as always, my cheerleader. She always believes in me even when there is much room for doubt.

Others listed in alphabetical order
"Captain Jason," cruise ship to Smith Island
Captain Terry Laird
Crisfield, Maryland
(410) 425-5931

"Chesapeake Breeze," cruise ship to Tangier Island
Capt. Linwood Bowis
Reedville, Virginia 22539
(804) 453-2628

Chester River Kayak Adventures
Liese Marshall and Jim Gillin
P.O. Box 189
5758 Main Street
Rock Hall, Maryland 21661
(410) 639-2001

Ewell Tide Inn
Teresa Seajack
Ewell on Smith Island
(888) 699-2141

Island Kayak, Inc.
Capt. Dan Vaughan
P.O. Box 357
Tilghman Island, Maryland 21671
(410) 886-2083
island-kayak.com

Pocomoke River Canoe Company
Barry Laws
312 N. Washington St.
Snow Hill, Maryland 21863
(410) 632-3961

Starrk Moon Kayaks
Brad Nelson
497 Cold Cabin Rd.
Delta, Pennsylvania 17314
(717) 456-7720
www.starrkmoon.com

Survival Products
Steve Corbett
1116 N. Salisbury Rd.
Salisbury, Maryland 21801
(410) 543-1244

Taylors Island Family Campground
Bruce Coulson
Taylors Island, Maryland 21669
(410) 397-3275

Acknowledgments

A book like this cannot be compiled without the help of scores of contributors: naturalists, outfitters, park managers, park rangers, locals, fishermen, historians, and many others who have rendered to me a portion of knowledge about the waterways in this region. Although my name is on the cover, it is really their book.

Provided information assistance, verification, affirmation or further technical assistance on some of these trails:

General information

- ◆ Audubon Society Field Guide to North American Mammals by John O. Whitaker, Jr.

- ◆ Audubon Society Field Guide to North American Trees by Elbert L. Little

- ◆ Audubon Society Field Guide to North American Wildflowers by William Niering and Nancy C. Olmstead

- ◆ Field Guide to the Birds East of the Rockies by Roger Tory Peterson

- ◆ Kathy Scott, grammarian

- ◆ Maryland and Delaware Canoe Trails by Ed Gertler

- ◆ Maryland Department of Natural Resources www.dnr.state.md.us

- ◆ Nature Guide to the Carolina Coast by Peter Meyer

- ◆ Ocracoke Wild by Pat Garber

- ◆ Sea Kayaking Along the Mid-Atlantic Coast by T. Venn

◆State of Delaware, Division of Parks and Recreation

Specific Sites

Appoquinimink River
◆http://h2osparc.wq.ncsu.edu/info/rcwp/deprof

Assateague
◆www.beach-net.com/chincoteague/refuge

Blackwater National Wildlife Refuge
◆"Blackwater National Wildlife Refuge," a brochure by the U.S. Fish and Wildlife Service

Bombay Hook National Wildlife Refuge
◆www.gorp.com/gorp/resource/us_nwr/de_bomba

Cape Henlopen State Park
◆Chris Bennett, Nature Center Manager
◆"Cape Henlopen State Park," a brochure by the Delaware Division of Parks and Recreation
◆www.beach-net.com

Conowingo Pond and Susquehanna Flats Area
◆Brad Nelson, Starrk Moon Kayaks
◆Steve Robinson, Starrk Moon Kayaks

Corkers Creek
◆"Bogiron Water Trails," a brochure by the Worcester County Department of Tourism

Eastern Neck Island National Wildlife Refuge
◆Mark Nelson, REI
◆http://northeast.fws.gov/md/esn

Elk Neck State Park
◆Deborah Algard
◆Ruth Ann Hoffman, Administrative Specialist
◆"Welcome to Elk Neck," a brochure by the Maryland Department of Natural Resources

Pocomoke River Area
- ◆Barry Laws, Pocomoke River Company
- ◆"The Pocomoke River," a brochure by the Worcester County Tourism Department
- ◆www.worc.lib.md.us/tourism/outdoor_rec/pocomoke

Point Lookout State Park
- ◆Christy Carter, Park Naturalist
- ◆Christina Wyrick, Park Naturalist
- ◆www.weta.com/potomac/regions/region13/detail4
- ◆www.somd.com/culture/stmarys/pt-lookout/index

Prime Hook National Wildlife Refuge
- ◆Frank Buck, Worker
- ◆Louise Katarba, Administrative Assistant
- ◆"Prime Hook National Wildlife Refuge," a brochure by the U.S. Department of the Interior
- ◆www.gorp.com/gorp/resource/us_nwr/de_prime

Salt Marsh Island Wildlife Management Area
- ◆www.dnr.state.md.us//publiclands/eastern/southmarsh

Smith Island
- ◆Janet Tyler, Manager, Smith Island Center
- ◆Rick Edmunds, Pastor of Methodist church
- ◆"Smith Island Maryland," a brochure by the Maryland Tourism Development Board
- ◆www.intercom.net/npo/smithisland
- ◆www.taoswolf.com/halfshell/crisfield

Sotterly Plantation
- ◆www.smithsonianmag.com/smithsonian/issues96/sep96/

Tangier Island
- ◆www.eaglesnest.net/tangier/tangier

Tilghman Island
- ◆www.tilghmanisland.com

◆www.elkneckstatepark.com

Janes Island State Park
◆"Janes Island State Park," a brochure by the Maryland Department of Natural Resources
◆www.dnr.state.md.us/publiclands/eastern/janesisland
◆www.shore-source.com/guides/somerset/sites/janesisl

Killens Pond State Park
◆Angela Wood, Park Interpreter

Little Assawoman Bay
◆Rob Gano, Regional Fish and Wildlife Manager
◆www.fenwickislandde.com

Marshyhope Creek
◆www.dnr.state.md/publiclands/eastern/idylwild

Martin National Wildlife
◆"Martin," a brochure by the U.S. Fish and Wildlife Service

Mason Neck State Park and National Wildlife Refuge
◆Cathryn Plum, Park Interpreter,
◆Anna Jordan, Chief Ranger
◆"Mason Neck State Park Guide," a brochure by the Department of Conservation and Recreation
◆www.patc.net/masn_sp
◆northeast.fws.gov/va/msn

Monie Creek
◆www.ezy.net/~davekel/monie

Nanjemoy Creek
◆www.tnc.org/infield/state/maryland/Profiles/Chesapeake

Nanticoke River
◆http://skipjack.net/le_shore/heritage/nanticok

Trap Pond State Park
◆Cathy Ruark, Administrative Assistant
◆"Trap Pond State Park," a brochure by the Delaware
   Division of Parks and Recreation

Tuckahoe State Park
◆www.dnr.state.md.us/publiclands/eastern/tuckahoe

Wicomico River
◆www.river-guide.com/pot119

Worlds End Creek
◆Mark Nelson, REI

**Provided information for "Notes" on flora or fauna of the
region and/or places of historic or scenic interest:**

Barn Owls
◆<u>A Field Guide to the Birds East of the Rockies</u> by Tory
   Peterson

Bayberry
◆www.viable-herbal.com/herbdesc/1bayberr

Blue Crabs
◆University of Delaware Sea Grant Marine Advisory
   Service

Canada Goose
◆www.canadagoose.com/lessons

Canvasback Duck
◆www.nysite.com/nature/fauna/canvas

Charles County, Maryland
◆www.govt.co.charles.md.us/tourism/birds/index

Clams
◆<u>Nature Guide to the North Carolina Coast</u> by Peter Meyer

Ducks
✦www.utm.edu/departments/ed/cece/ducks

DuPont Family
✦<u>World Book Encyclopedia</u>

Havre de Grace
✦www.hardfordchamber.com/tourist/info

Herons
✦<u>Nature Guide to the North Atlantic Coast</u> by Peter Meyer

Horseshoe Crabs
✦"The Horseshoe Crab," a brochure by the Delaware Division of Parks and Recreation
✦www.beach-net.com/horseshoe/Bayhorsecrab

Mistletoe
✦www.encarta.msn.com/find/concise.asp?z

Mosquitos
✦<u>Ocracoke Wild</u> by Pat Garber

Muskrats, Beavers, and River Otters
✦<u>The Audubon Society Field Guide to North American Mammals</u> by Jack Whitaker, Jr.

Ospreys
✦www.pressplus.com/content/birds/ospreytower
✦www.savethepeconicbays.org/kids/southampton/justfact
✦www.salamander.com/~rrp/ospreys

Skipjacks
✦www.geocities.com/~skipjacksloop

Shorebirds
✦"Delaware Bay Shorebirds" by the Delaware Department of Natural Resources and Environmental Control

Sub-aquatic Plants
+ "Life in the Shallows" by the U.S. Fish and Wildlife Service

Tundra Swans
+ www.bsc-eoc.org/swans/swans

Water lilies
+ <u>Audubon Society Field Guide to North American Wildflowers</u> by William Niering and Nancy C. Olmstead

Campground locations:

Maryland
+ www.gocampingamerica.com/directory/maryland
+ www.kiz.com/campnet/html/cluborg/mac

Delaware
+ www.delmarweb.com/delaware/campground
+ www.happycamping.com/de
+ www.rvpark.com/del

Delaware and Maryland combined
+ www.bigyellow.com
+ www.disdirectory.com/camping
+ www.rvclassified.com/campgrnd

Ferry Information

To Smith Island
From Crisfield
> "Island Princess", "Island Belle II" (410)968-3206
> "The Captain Tyler II" (410) 425-2771
> "The Captain Jason I and II" (410) 425-5931
> > *will take boats*
>
> "The Sunrise" (888) 699-2141
> > *will take boats*

From Reedville, VA
> "Spirit of Chesapeake" (804) 453-3430

To Tangier Island
From Crisfield
> Tangier Island Cruises 301-968-2338
> Tangier Mail and Freight Service 757-891-2240
> > *will take boats*

From Reedville
> Tangier Cruises 804-333-4656

From Onancock
> Hopkins and Brothers Store 804-787-8220